DECORATING
MADE SIMPLE

DECORATING MADE SIMPLE

MARY JEAN ALEXANDER

Author of *Decorating Begins With You*

Past-President of The Decorators' Club Inc., New York City

Member of the American Institute of Interior Designers

Former faculty member of the Art School of Pratt Institute and the

Parsons School of Design

Drawings by

LYMAN MARTIN

MADE SIMPLE BOOKS
DOUBLEDAY & COMPANY, INC.
GARDEN CITY, NEW YORK

Library of Congress Catalog Card Number 64–13823
Copyright © 1964 by Doubleday & Company, Inc.
All Rights Reserved
Printed in the United States of America

CONTENTS

Chapter One   You and Your Home   1

What Kind of a Home Do You Really Want?   1
Your Home Should Be the Sum of Your Needs + Your Taste + Good Design   3

Chapter Two   Guide to Design Terms   5

Design Vocabulary   5
Unity   5
Line and Form   8
Scale and Proportion   14
Balance   17
Rhythm   19
Emphasis   21
Contrast   22
Variety   23
Texture   23
Pattern   24
Design, Ornament, and Decoration   25
The Goal: Combine Your Taste with Function and Good Design   26

Chapter Three   Where Do You Start?   27

The Importance of a General Plan   27
Steps to Sound Planning   27
The Floor Plan   29
Arranging Your Furniture   35
Function—Room by Room   42
Now You Have Started   47

Chapter Four   Understanding Color   49

General Facts About Color   49
Make Your Own Color Chart   50
Qualities of Color   52
Types of Color Schemes   53
Color Names of Pigments   53
Effects of Color on a Room   54
Summary   56

Chapter Five   Floors and Floor Coverings   59

    Start with the Floor   59
    Hard-surface Flooring   60
    Soft Floor Coverings   63

Chapter Six   Walls and Wall Coverings   77

    The Importance of Careful Planning   77
    Make the Most of Your Architecture   77
    General Design Suggestions   79
    Painted Walls   81
    Wall Coverings   82
    Other Wall Treatments   87

Chapter Seven   Windows   89

    Choose the Right Window Treatment   89
    Function, and Kinds of Windows   89
    Methods of Controlling Daylight   91
    Exterior Appearance   92
    Curtains   92
    Summary   100

Chapter Eight   Fabrics

    Kinds of Fabrics   103
    Woven Fabrics   103
    Fibers   103
    Knit Fabrics   104
    Felted Fabrics   106
    Vinyl Fabrics   106
    Special Processes   107
    When Buying Fabrics   107
    Be Sure to Choose the Right Fabrics   107
                                                                           108

Chapter Nine   Furniture   109

    Plan Your Buying Thoughtfully   109
    Two Kinds of Furniture   109
    Case Goods   109
    Upholstered Furniture   116
    Tips on Looking for Furniture   118

Chapter Ten   Accessories—Their Importance, Selection, and Use   121

    What Are Accessories—and Why Have Them?   121
    Using Accessories   122
    Selecting Accessories   129
    Placing Accessories   130
    Summary   131

Chapter Eleven   Lighting and Equipment

    Lighting   133
    Kitchens   133
    Television   138
                                                                           140

Chapter Twelve **A Short History of Interior Design** 143

    Italy 144
    France 146
    England 156
    United States 166

Glossary 172

Index 179

DECORATING
MADE SIMPLE

CHAPTER ONE

YOU AND YOUR HOME

WHAT KIND OF A HOME DO YOU REALLY WANT?

Whether you live in a large house or a tiny apartment; on a farm, in town or in the city, if you are interested in improving the home you have, or lucky enough to be getting a new one, the first thing to do is take the time to figure out exactly the home you would like to have. The chances are that you have intermittently given the matter some thought. If so, you have probably fallen in love with a few individual pieces of furniture or some particular fabric or wallpaper.

But, have you thought about your home as a whole—in its entirety—as the sum total of *all* its parts? Until you have done this, thoughtfully and painstakingly, you aren't likely to really know what kind of a home you want.

Throughout the process of thinking about your home and planning its improvement, your own tastes will be back of all of your ideas. They should be. The first and perhaps the most important requirement for any choice is your personal reaction to it. This is your home. Everything in it, as far as practically possible, should please you and should reflect your personality. On the other hand, you want it to appear attractive and tasteful to others. How do you accomplish both of these ends?

Check Your Own Home First. Start by figuring out what you do like. Just as important, know what you don't like. Go through your own home and make a list of the things in your house that you really like. Be thoughtful, thorough, and honest. You may include a piece of furniture (probably several), a fabric, rug, wallpaper, picture, accessory—anything that is there that contributes

some quality that you like. Then, just as carefully, make a list of all the things that you wish weren't there.

Observe Other Homes. Outside of your own home, train yourself to observe. There are many beautiful objects to be seen, in both expected and unexpected places. Look at them. As you go in and out of the homes of friends, take a little time to observe. If something appeals to you, figure out exactly what it is and why you like it. If you have an opportunity to take a tour of homes that are supposed to be either especially interesting or particularly well designed, observe—and *really* see what you are looking at. A quick glance may satisfy your curiosity as to how these people live, but only careful observation of the effects you really like will help you in your own planning.

Visit Model Rooms. Ideas are a dime a dozen in any department store where model rooms have been set up. They may not all be good ideas, but take your time to see and evaluate them. Try to go as soon as possible after the rooms have been opened to the public and early in the day, or any time when the store is not crowded. If you attend any kind of a home-furnishings show, make a practice of really seeing what's there and thinking about it. Take some kind of small notebook and keep as many notes as possible. If you can't take notes there, as soon as you get home, jot down any ideas that appealed to you, while they are fresh in your mind.

Taste. Perhaps you think you have good taste —and do. You may think you don't have it and wish you did. You may not have it and think you do, or you may even have it and think you don't. Taste is a tricky business. But no matter at what level you start, and regardless of your own opinion of your taste, if you are interested enough to try, you can improve and develop your taste. Good taste is nothing more than enlightened choice. The more knowledge you acquire, the more carefully you observe and analyze what you see, the faster your conclusions will lead your taste level to develop in the right direction—up. But you can't shilly-shally. You must really look and see; know what you've seen, and decide what you like. It is absolutely essential for you to make decisions as to what you like or dislike and evolve some definite ideas about the kind of a home you want.

How Do You Live? The way you live will certainly have a lot to do with your choice of the kind of home you want. Ask and answer some questions for yourself. Are you and your family fond of hearty living—apt to need strong fabrics and furniture? Do you require space and equipment for outdoor living? What does the climate suggest where your activities are concerned? Is music important to all or part of the family? Do you like games? If so, are they the kind where you sit, or move around? Do you need spaces that are separated from activities, where members of the family can read, write, or quietly carry on private enterprises? Do you entertain a lot? If you will make a list of questions about the way you live—or would like to live—and answer them, it can be very enlightening. When you've finished, consult the other members of the family.

If there is too much disagreement, take a long-range view and don't try to compromise and please everyone. There are times when you can't be all things to all people, so just do the best you can. Careful planning will make your best much better.

Keep a Scrapbook of Ideas. A scrapbook is an aid to observing and analyzing, because it will help you to formulate your own ideas. It can provide clues that will also help you to understand the whys of what you like or don't like. Start now, if you haven't already, to collect photos and sketches, in black and white or color. Include everything, from any source at all, that you really like. Keep your pictures carefully sorted, either in a scrapbook or a file. They are much more useful if they are easy to refer to.

When you try to recall some special effect that you liked, or some particularly handsome piece of furniture that you've seen, you won't have to rack your brain. You have only to go to your file and find the picture. Then there's no doubt about it. One picture is worth a dozen descriptions if you want to explain an idea. And when you can't quite remember what it was you liked so much (it often happens, even though you *know* there was *something*), there is no substitute for a picture.

Your picture collection can be useful in another way—in helping you to gain an understanding of your own likes and dislikes. You can pore over these pictures, analyzing the things you like, taking all the time you need. Try to understand why you like them. Then figure out what it is in each that you find so satisfactory and you will probably find that some pictures have certain qualities in common that appeal to you. This can mean the beginning of a trend in your taste that will speed up its development.

If you persist in asking yourself why you like some effects especially and can find the answer, and decide what they do have in common (not always easy), usually some consistent qualities will emerge. You may discover that you can't stand a lot of fussy things together or that you simply love controlled clutter. You may be happiest with an elegant window treatment, a severely tailored one, or ruffled curtains. You will surely make some discoveries about yourself and your tastes if you will collect pictures that you like and follow through on a study of them.

Learn To Make Decisions. So, you are now approaching a point where you begin to know and understand what you like and why. The next big step is to learn to make decisions. Naturally, you should make the right ones—a truism if ever there was one. But, it is better to make the wrong one than to keep right on procrastinating, unable to come to one at all. The fewer wrong ones, the better, of course. But, don't let it upset you if you do make a mistake. What you must do, then, is turn it into a blessing. Keep right on analyzing. How, where, and why did you go wrong? When you have figured out the answer to these questions, you aren't likely to make the same mistake again. Almost certainly, the next time you will be more thorough in your thinking, and on the basis of your thoroughness and your past mistake, the chances are you will make the right decision.

Practice making up your mind. Don't make

decisions under pressure just to get things moving. Start by carefully exploring the situation and all the requirements that should be met. Then consider possible alternatives to a good solution —and decide. Some people can't—or don't—sort out their ideas and the facts. They seem to develop a chronic inability to make up their minds, and their homes show it. You've seen these homes, they look as though someone had a different idea every time anything was added to a room. The confused hodgepodge that results from this approach can be avoided with a little care and thought.

Chronic indecision is not to be confused with a problem that arises when you need to choose between two objects or ideas, either of which would be suitable and both of which have been given careful consideration. Take plenty of time to think this over, then make a decision and go ahead. But don't let yourself get the horrible habit of indecision.

Your Home Should Be the Sum of Your Needs + Your Taste + Good Design

Keep It Personal. As you learn, through observing, analyzing, and experimenting, to understand why you like certain things and how to make up your mind about them, keep right on expressing your own personality. Your personal whims will be back of your tastes, and that is as it should be. Your instinctive inclinations may not all be supercharged with brilliant design talent. But when you get what you think is a bright idea, give it a chance. It may turn out to be the big inspiration that will make it possible to achieve the exact effect you have been yearning for. Try to evaluate it impersonally. Be really objective, if possible. But don't discourage yourself from having as many ideas as you can—based on your personal likes.

As you continue to observe and analyze and begin to understand why certain effects are good design and others aren't, you gradually become sensitive to more and more combinations of color and design. Your aesthetic sense becomes sharper, you can appreciate increasingly more subtle combinations, and your standards of taste improve. You will gradually be able to express your own individual ideas in your home—in good taste.

Beauty and Function Are of Equal Importance. The most beautiful chair in the world is a failure if it isn't practical to sit in, and the most comfortable chair a failure if it is ugly. The twin aims of good decorating and design are beauty and proper function. Which comes first? At one time, one may precede the other; the next time, the order will be reversed. You will have to decide which to place first before you start your planning. They are equally important and both absolutely essential to good design. Unless the finished results look well and work, they won't reflect good decorating.

You and Your Home. You've learned now how to discover your own taste and once it's discovered, how to develop it. And you've learned to study carefully and to determine what you and your family need in your home. Your taste and your needs govern what you want. The succeeding chapters will help to show you *how* to achieve it and to assure its quality of design.

CHAPTER TWO

GUIDE TO DESIGN TERMS

DESIGN VOCABULARY

You've started to learn, in a sensible and realistic way, what kind of home you want. You have taken a few steps—perhaps more—on the path to developing your own good taste, based on your individual ideas. You are discovering what you like and don't like by consciously directed observation and careful analysis. The next step is to put your accumulating knowledge to work.

In order to do this, you must know and thoroughly understand the language of design and decoration. Most of the terms will seem familiar. But unless you can define them precisely, and can understand the way they are used, here, you won't be able to use them. In order to apply them later, you must comprehend each one, now.

Certain basic art principles and elements underlie all good design. If you use them properly, you can create a room that will look the way you want it to. If you misuse them, you will find yourself making mistakes without knowing why or how you are making them. These few principles apply to all forms of design and are not difficult to understand or to use. They are: unity, line, form, scale, proportion, balance, rhythm, emphasis, contrast, variety, texture, pattern, and ornament. In addition, underlying all and absolutely necessary to good interior design, is function. No matter how beautiful a room may look, unless it truly fulfills its function, it is not good design. Remember that the most beautiful piece of furniture in the world is a failure unless it is practical to use.

UNITY

A well-designed room must have unity. The principle of unity encompasses all the other principles and elements, and it is most important to understand just what it is. Unity requires an arrangement of parts that produces a single and orderly whole that is aesthetically pleasing. In a room, unity also requires that functional needs be fulfilled. Every part of a room and every object in it should fulfill its function, add to the appearance, and contribute to the total effect.

No matter how perfect an individual object, unless it appears to add to the general effect and seems to belong with everything else in the room, it will destroy the unity. A heavy table, of the style used in an Early American home, would be totally out of place in an eighteenth-century room; but used in the right place, it would add to the design. To achieve unity, you must consider size, shape, color, texture, and general feeling of an object in relation to everything else in the room. The rug, the wallpaper, the furniture and its coverings, the curtains, lamps, pictures, and other accessories—all must appear at home together.

To achieve unity in a room it isn't necessary to limit yourself to one wood finish, to the same fabric, or even to a period of design, as long as your furnishings seem to go together. A Colonial room doesn't have to have a Williamsburg paper, nor a modern room an abstract painting. But everything that goes into a room should work toward a unified effect. If you start out planning a cool, uncluttered modern room, you can't bring in some ruffled curtains or a flowered chintz arm-

Fig. 1 *Above* an Early American table completely out of place. *Below* used appropriately.

Fig. 2 Ruffles destroy the unity of *this* room.

chair with a flounce and expect to preserve the desired effect.

If there is one main theme built around a dominant center of interest, such as a painting, a fireplace, or a beautiful piece of furniture, it will help to achieve unity. All of the other design, in varying degrees of strength, gives support to the theme. The furniture, the wall and floor treatment, the accessories, color and any pattern must have in common some quality of purpose and appearance. Each depends on the others and in an orderly way contributes its share to the whole. No element can be taken away or added, without sacrificing the basic design idea.

This doesn't mean that you can't ever change anything. If you want to change a room that already has unity, it is possible to plan additions or replacements in such a way that you will create a new unity. But move carefully, remembering that no object, no matter how beautiful, is an addition to a room unless it takes its place as a part of the complete, orderly unit.

In a room that has unity, your eye won't be tempted to jump from one place to another. Unity assures a sense of order which gives you a feeling of repose, and you relax. There is a consistency of sizes and shapes, a harmony of color and pattern. Look around your rooms. Do they have this quality? If they don't, try arranging and adjusting the individual parts and see if you can't create a peaceful whole.

Fig. 3 A room carefully planned around a center of interest.

LINE AND FORM

Line and form are so entirely taken for granted that definition seems unnecessary. But in a room they are usually more complicated than they seem. Line, as used in designing a room, is more important than any other element except color. A line can be defined, for this purpose, as a long, thin mark, which may, when it encloses a space, become an outline or a contour. Forms are made by lines, but lines don't always make forms.

There are two general kinds of lines—straight and curved. Straight lines are more severe than curved lines and give a feeling of strength. They may be vertical, horizontal, or diagonal. Vertical lines are strong and direct. They suggest the vertical supports used in building and have a structural feeling. They may be more suitable for a formal effect than curved lines. Vertical lines, whether in doorways, windows or other architectural features, wallpaper, or furnishings, suggest height in a room. With low ceilings the general rule in most rooms being built today, it is impor-tant to understand how vertical lines can be used to make a room appear higher.

Horizontal lines are more tranquil, not as strong as vertical lines, and fundamentally more restful. Architecturally, horizontal lines often provide relief from strong vertical lines. Horizontal lines in a room can be provided by tables, benches, a desk, chair, or sofa, by the top of a doorway, window, or fireplace. It has been suggested that the qualities of vertical and horizontal lines are emotional ones, based on the fact that when man is in action, he is usually vertical, and when resting, horizontal.

Diagonal lines are the trickiest ones to use. They seem to be pointing into space and unless they are decisively stopped, they are likely to keep the eye moving. Diagonal lines are emphatically lines of action and, not properly controlled, they may be annoying. A herringbone pattern, which consists of diagonal lines meeting in Vs, makes a good design, since the lines meet, thereby completing each other and avoiding a feeling of restlessness. If diagonal lines are too dominant

Fig. 4 *Above* too many verticals. *Below* verticals used properly.

in a room—in the arrangement of one wall, for instance—they disrupt the basic structural form and destroy the unity of the room. Don't give them up as being too difficult. If you like them, use them. But be sure to control them; don't let them get away from you.

The two kinds of curved lines are mathematical and freehand. Any curved lines, but especially freehand ones, are gayer and more fun than straight lines. Good curved lines are graceful, soft, and subtle. A mathematical curve is made with an instrument, from any part of the arc of a circle or an ellipse. The curve made from the arc of a circle is less subtle and lacks variety. The arc of the ellipse allows for more variety, changing its direction at different points of the circumference.

The freehand curves, when beautifully drawn or formed, have great subtlety and there is no end to their variety. But, there is a big difference between the beautiful ones and those that are ordinary. One of the best ways to see the contrast is to place a Louis XV chair beside a Victorian chair (if this isn't possible, use pictures) and study the curves. The curves in the Victorian chair were not done with the taste and care shown in the designs of the Louis XV period and are definitely inferior to them. Good freehand curves give a feeling of airiness, but they haven't the appearance of strength. Their use must be planned in relation to straight lines, or they may seem to be weak rather than airy.

Fig. 5 *Above* horizontals overemphasized. *Below* used properly.

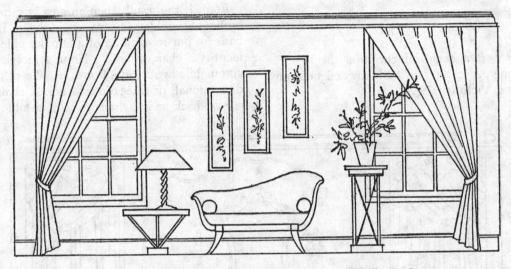

Fig. 6 *Above* diagonals overused. *Below* used effectively.

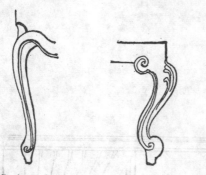

Fig. 7 *Left* a beautiful curve on the leg of a Louis XV chair. *Right* a badly designed curve on a Victorian leg.

Too many curved lines in a room produce a restless effect. It isn't too difficult to recognize this fault when it appears. The best way to correct it is to strengthen the straight lines or to eliminate some of the curved ones. On the other hand, in a room where there are too many straight lines, curved lines are useful to relieve stiffness.

Form is the result when an area is surrounded by lines assembled to represent a shape. It is the basis for our recognition of a familiar object. We identify a chair, a desk, a lamp, a bicycle, or an automobile by its form. Forms may be either two-dimensional, or three-dimensional. A chair has a curved back or leg; the surface of a table makes

Fig. 8 *Above* too many curves. *Below* rectangular panes in the french doors, straight-hanging curtains, and fewer curves in furniture provide a better combination of straight and curved lines.

a straight line. Each view of an object may give a different impression of the lines that compose it—of its form. Form is not as quickly perceived as color because it requires an intellectual response; color a more emotional one.

Straight lines form squares, rectangles, and triangles of various sizes and shapes. A square completes itself, giving a feeling of solidarity, but too many in a design may become monotonous. Square rooms are not common and are more difficult to decorate agreeably than other rectangular shapes. In the past, rooms were usually rectangles of varying proportions. There are still many rectangular rooms being built, but in general, there is more variety in the shape of rooms today, more combinations of straight and curved forms. An isosceles triangle with its two equal sides suggests balance and is frequently found in arrangements of furniture or wall designs. Other kinds of triangles are more difficult to use and should be avoided unless they can be used without destroying the unity of a room.

A circle or an oval has movement, but both complete themselves, and are not restless. An oval, not surprisingly, has more subtlety than a

circle. When used against a rectangular form, either a circle or an oval must be placed with care or the contrast will create too much pattern. Cir-

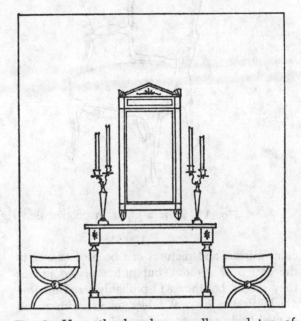

Fig. 9 Here, the benches, candles, and top of the mirror form a balanced isosceles triangle.

Fig. 10 *Left* circle well integrated in a rectangle. *Right* floating with no connection.

Fig. 11 *Left* a chair in good scale. *Right* an example of bad scale in a chair.

cular mirrors and pictures can be used to add to the design of a room, but unless placed just as they should be, they will probably stand out too much. Round or oval tables, chairs with round or oval backs or seats, and round or oval rugs can be used to soften and relieve stiffness in a room with too many straight lines.

SCALE AND PROPORTION

Scale and proportion are both relative qualities, and it is difficult to separate them. It is better if you don't. Try to understand them together. Scale—basically, the size relationship—means the relationship of each part of an object to another part and to the whole. Proportion means the

shape of one area in relation to the whole that contains it.

Scale denotes size in comparison to what you are used to. Proportion, to be good, requires that the relations between the shapes of the parts of a unit—whether it is a single piece, a composition of objects, or a whole room—are pleasing. For example, a picture frame is properly proportioned if the width has the right relationship to the height. The frame is properly scaled if it is the right size for the picture it frames—not too small or too large.

Since all interiors are planned for the use of human beings, the rooms and everything in them should be scaled to the size of the average human figure. Good scale requires that all parts of an object be related, as to size, in a satisfying way—to each other, to the object as a whole, every other object in the room, and the room itself. Every

Fig. 12 *From left to right:* a badly scaled frame, a badly proportioned frame, a frame in good scale and proper proportion for this picture.

Fig. 13 *Above* a room with badly scaled forms. *Below* a room designed in good scale.

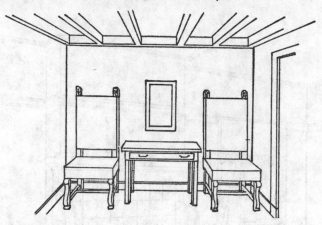

Fig. 14 *Above* chairs out of scale with room. *Below* room and chairs in proper
scale for each other.

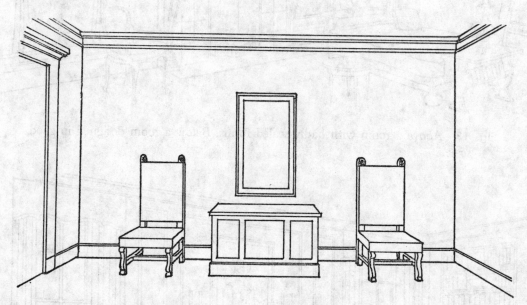

single thing in a room will seem large or small in comparison or contrast to the other objects. A large chair which looks all right in a large room will appear to be too heavy in a small room; while a chair that is small in scale may seem lost in a large room.

Good proportion requires all forms to be pleasingly related. It is very important to unity. The proportions of a room are good if the windows and doors seem right within their walls and if the wall sizes—height and width—are agreeable together. Any area must look well within its containing shape—the relationship of the rug to the floor, a piece or a group of furniture to the wall against which it stands, or the pattern used on a chair to the chair.

The law of the ancient Greeks on proportion is generally accepted as a consistently sound one. Used together, two areas have the most successful effect if one is more than one half and less than two thirds of the other. Areas should be sufficiently alike to have something in common and different enough to be interesting. So arranged, they will have a subtlety of interest and a beauty not to be found in identical pieces.

Fig. 15 *Above* bad proportion. *Below* good proportion.

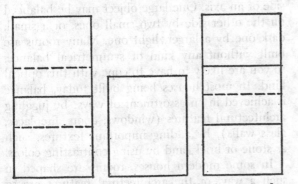

Fig. 16 The area in the middle is more than half, less than two thirds the size of the others.

BALANCE

Balance is the principle of good design, in a room, that assures a sense of repose or equilibrium. Balance is a harmonious relation of parts, giving the appearance of equal distribution on either side of a focal point or line. Properly used in a room, balance creates a sense of rest and a feeling of completion. Every element of a room and every object in it must be considered where balance is concerned. Areas, color, forms, texture, pattern, and lighting are all part of balance. No room without balance will have unity.

There are two basic kinds of balance: symmetrical and asymmetrical, or optical. Symmetrical

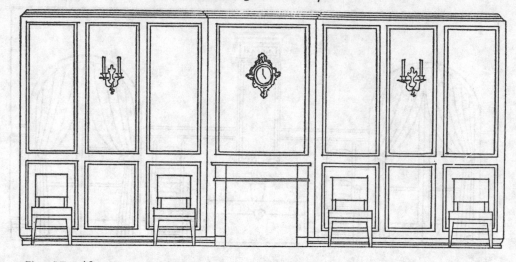

Fig. 17 *Above* symmetrical balance that is repetitious and uninteresting. *Below* symmetrical balance well used.

balance results when objects of similar design and equal weight or size are placed on either side of an axis, at an equal distance from it. Symmetrical balance in a room is dignified and often used in formal rooms. It is restrained and reflects intelligence rather than imagination. It can create beautiful effects, but may lack warmth. Most of the superb eighteenth-century rooms designed in France, England, and America were symmetrical in their wall design.

If you want a more casual room, the asymmetrical or optical balance may suit you better. It is more subtle and spontaneous, more difficult to use well, but capable of more exciting results than symmetrical balance. It permits more variety and allows for more personal expression. A sense of balance is created by arranging two groups of ob-

jects of different size, shape, or color, on either side of an axis. One large object may be balanced on the other side by two small ones, or a small, dark one by a larger, light one. Many rooms are built without any kind of symmetrical balance, so you are likely to have to cope with this optical kind. In most houses being built today, balance is achieved in an assortment of ways: by juggling architectural features (windows, doors, fireplaces, glass walls), by adding important textures, such as stone or brick, and by using contrasting colors.

In some modern houses, rooms are shaped in such a way, or the architectural features are so placed that a third and less common kind of balance may be required. In a room that is round or oval, or is built around an important feature, such as a fireplace, in or near the center, a radial

Fig. 18 *Above* a poor example of asymmetrical balance of door, furniture, and paintings. *Below* a good example.

symmetry may be needed to achieve balance. It would have to be a kind of asymmetric balance that focuses on the center of the room as the point of dominant interest. If you have this kind of room, don't let other areas of the room compete with the center of interest, which should be built up, with all other design supporting it. Unless it is, the room will appear to be going in all directions, will be restless, and lack unity.

RHYTHM

The arrangement of line and form in a room that forces the eye to move from one place to another is movement. Rhythm supplies the discipline that controls the movement and guides the eye so it will see the parts of the room in the way dictated by the design. Contrast and variety are both part of rhythm, but must be kept under careful control. Rhythmic movement helps the eye to flow, rather than jump, from one object to another. Rhythm, although not very tangible, is essential to good design.

The commonest kind of rhythm is repetition—of line, form, pattern, or color. It is marked by a regular recurrence of shapes, pattern, or accents, separated by equal spaces. An allover pattern of circles, squares, or other forms in wallpapers and fabrics is a frequently used example of rhythm by repetition. The way color is used has a definite effect on the rhythm. Close values and contrasting values have an opposite effect. Colors that

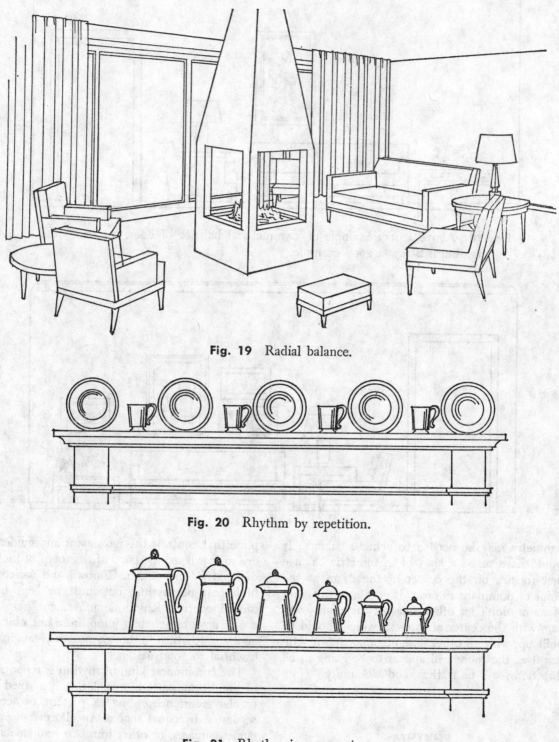

Fig. 19 Radial balance.

Fig. 20 Rhythm by repetition.

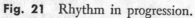

Fig. 21 Rhythm in progression.

Fig. 22 *Above* a random arrangement without a center of interest. *Below* furniture well grouped, here focusing on the window.

are close together have little effect on the rhythm, while strong contrasts in color may be as important as the pattern itself. This regular repetition in rhythm is easy to use but may lack subtlety, since it has little variety.

Progressive rhythm, a gradually increasing or decreasing change in size, can be used effectively and dramatically. This type of rhythm permits the use of more originality, has more strength, and is more dynamic than repetition. It is more difficult to use successfully and unless carefully planned may have the look of a stepladder. The progression may be of size, direction, or color. Sizes may go from large to small, or vice versa; lines from vertical to horizontal; and colors from a strong to a soft value of one color, such as blue, through blue-green to green. Progressive rhythm carries the eye more daringly. If you can use it successfully, it will combine the elements of the room into a unit, avoiding the restless feeling of incompletion that unregulated movement may produce.

EMPHASIS

Emphasis, contrast, and variety are three important, related aspects of good interior design. The proper use of emphasis brings order to the

Fig. 23 *Above* contrast well used. *Below* contrast poorly used.

various elements and helps to make a room unified. The main scheme of a room must be built around a dominant center of interest. If everything in a room—or even several important objects—are of equal importance, there is a feeling of competition and a lack of co-ordination. One of the first things to decide when you are planning a room is what you are featuring as the center of interest. This must be sufficiently emphasized so that everything else in the room takes its right place in the composition as a whole, assuring unity.

CONTRAST

A basic ingredient of emphasis is contrast, which means the opposition of things or qualities, especially those used next to each other. Contrast may mean horizontal lines emphasizing vertical ones; or curved lines against straight ones. It may mean strong colors against muted ones, or complements used together; smooth surfaces against rough textures. The purpose of contrast is to make one thing stand out more sharply against another and thus be more important to

Fig. 24 *Above* too much variety. *Below* interesting variety.

the design. Contrasts must be carefully planned so as to stay within the limits of unity in a room. Used without moderation, they may give some emotional satisfaction (watch out for this—it is a very temporary satisfaction), but they will almost certainly disrupt the feeling of unity and make the room restless.

VARIETY

Variety is another ingredient of emphasis. It is the lack of sameness. It provides the spice that makes the difference between a pleasant room and an interesting or exciting one. Variety can

provide vitality; but too much of it, like too much spice, will ruin the total effect. Contrast and variety must both be used with restraint and in just the needed amount.

TEXTURE

Texture refers to the surface quality of an object—its roughness or smoothness. It is known primarily through the sense of touch, but while it is basically tactile, through its use today it has also become a visual quality. The light and shadow of a nubby fabric or the cool, shiny look of marble have both a tactile and a visual effect.

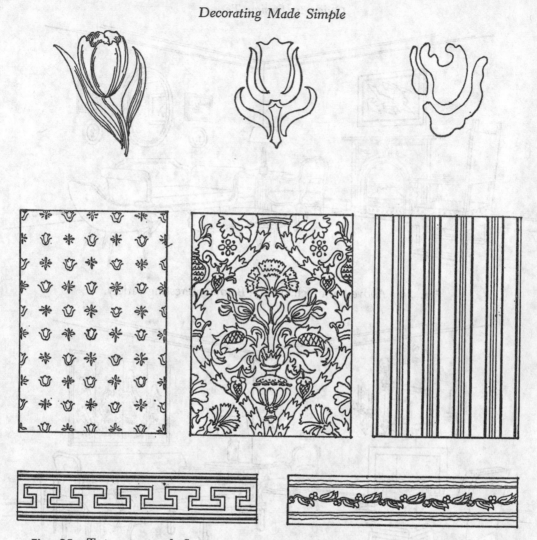

Fig. 25 *Top* a natural flower, conventionalized flower, and abstract design. *Center* three types of pattern. *Bottom* ornamental bands.

Texture may seem to change a color. A nubby fabric and a smooth one may seem to be the same color when lying flat, side by side. In use they will look quite different. The nubby fabric has many shadows, making it darker, while the shiny one reflects light and appears lighter. Keep this in mind when choosing colors and be sure to consider exactly how and where the texture will be used.

Every material has its own texture—very rough, rough, smooth, shiny, soft, harsh—or somewhere in between. In addition, in many designs today, for fabrics, wall, and floor coverings, an illusion of texture makes a smooth surface appear to be textured. A combination of different textures offers an extra and interesting ingredient for use in designing a room. Different textures can also be used together in a single object or piece of furniture to enhance the appearance, and an exciting and dramatic room can be designed in a single color, featuring textures as the main design element.

PATTERN

Pattern is two-dimensional or three-dimensional ornament put together in an orderly arrangement of motifs. While all pattern is ornament, all ornament is not pattern. Motifs used for patterns may be natural, conventionalized,

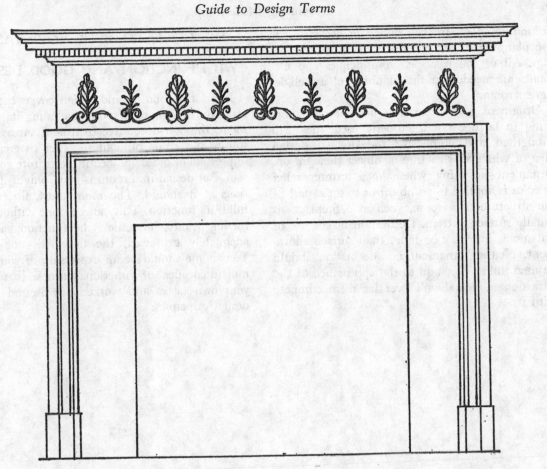

Fig. 26 Decoration used on a fireplace.

abstract, or imaginary. When patterns copy the forms of nature as accurately as possible, they are described as natural (or realistic). When a motif is taken from nature and then adapted and simplified to fit its use in the design, it is called conventionalized. Abstract patterns may be made from free forms or various combinations of geometric forms. If the elements of the pattern are not related to nature in any way, but are invented by the designer, they are called imaginary.

Types of patterns include small allover repeats, large-scale complicated motifs either traditional or abstract, various kinds of stripes, and borders. The allover repeats are usually on a plain ground, the others may be used against a plain ground or a small allover pattern. Proper use of pattern depends on the principles of good design. When you make your selection, be especially careful about scale and rhythm—and, of course, color. Pattern has movement and must be used so it will flow with, not against, the rhythm of the room. Don't let any of your pattern compete with the center of interest in a room. You may need to try a fairly large sample in the room in order to be sure. The variety of patterned textiles, wall, and floor coverings to be had in natural, conventional, and abstract patterns and simulated materials that provide design, is almost unlimited. It offers a very wide choice. The wider the choice, the greater your responsibility to make yours the right one.

DESIGN, ORNAMENT, AND DECORATION

The terms design, ornament, and decoration are commonly used, but not always clearly or accurately. Here, design means the creation of a plan for the making of a finished room or any object that goes into it. It requires a choice of line, space, form, and color to arrange a unified decorative effect. Interior design or decoration is the planning of any interior and all its furnishings. All of the basic-design principles and elements are needed in the planning of a well-designed room.

Ornament and decoration both imply something to be decorated. Properly used, they will strengthen and emphasize the original design idea of whatever structure or object they are on. Ornament—resulting when line, texture, relief or color is applied to an object or to some part of the structure of a room, such as a fireplace—is usually surface pattern. Decoration makes use of ornament, but may be more than surface adornment. Neither ornament nor decoration should be used unless they add to the appearance of the basic-design idea. Don't ever let them compete with it.

THE GOAL: COMBINE YOUR TASTE WITH FUNCTION AND GOOD DESIGN

Interior decoration and design covers the planning and design of a room, including its adornment, through decorative treatment. Areas, lines, forms, and color brought together to create an impression of order and beauty constitute good design. But design in a room is good only if it functions as it should. The room must, first of all, fulfill its function. This can be done without sacrificing beauty, but unless the functional idea is adequately expressed, the design is not good. Your home should be an expression of your own individual idea of functional fitness, based on your own tastes and worked out around sound design principles.

CHAPTER THREE

WHERE DO YOU START?

THE IMPORTANCE OF A GENERAL PLAN

You can have a home that satisfies you, and that will also satisfy all the members of your family. Your home can be one in which everyone can carry on his own activities without annoying the others (within limits—no snare drums!) and can experience the satisfaction of living in a place that is comfortable, functional, and attractive. In order to do this and to be sure of supplying the two qualities absolutely necessary to such a home—usefulness and beauty—you will have to start at the beginning. This doesn't mean that you have to start from scratch and throw away anything you have that you like, but it does mean that you will have a complete over-all plan and budget. Make your plan on the basis of your present circumstances and proceed from there.

Method of Approach. The over-all plan and the steps that follow it provide the groundwork for your entire decorating scheme, so work them out carefully and as completely as possible. The first step in decorating a room is to determine its function, what will be done there; the second is to list the equipment required, (appliances, a piano, beds, or whatever is *necessary*). Next is the most enjoyable part: working out your ideal plan, using your ideas, and including all the individual touches you can imagine. This is followed, naturally, by the stark reality of budgeting. Then, armed with a revised and a more realistic list, you can start to shop for some basic purchases. Before you make final decisions, you will work out a detailed floor plan, on which you will arrange the furniture, placing each piece to its best advantage.

Include the Family. Whether you are simply redecorating the living room, remodeling the attic into a room, or building an entire house, include all members of the family in organizing your plan. Alert each one and ask him to give some serious thought to the project. The more ideas you collect to work with—and almost certainly everyone who can talk will offer some—the better chance you have of coming up with the best solution for all concerned.

STEPS TO SOUND PLANNING

What to Consider First. While the thinking is going on and the suggestions coming in, sit down and organize your own ideas. Don't worry about color at the beginning; don't even try to select exact pieces of furniture, curtains, or rugs. Decide what kind of room you want. Is it to be formal or informal, restful or gay?

Then list the activities that will take place there. Activities can require a lot of movement (Ping-Pong) or virtually none (knitting), but either kind can be noisy or quiet. Listening to music, watching a play on television, or playing cards can all be done with very little movement, but may make enough noise to bother anyone within hearing distance who isn't interested. Reading, conversation, or sleeping can't be done very well in an area that is too close to any noisy activity. The amount of movement and noise you anticipate in an area must be given important consideration in your planning. Noisy, lively activities require the most space; noisy ones with little motion are next; and those that are quiet in every way take the least.

Once you have determined what kind of activities your spaces must provide for, you can plan furnishings and special equipment accordingly. For instance, a lavatory should be located near a play or recreation room. Any room where snacks or refreshments are frequently served should either be convenient to the kitchen or have some kind of serving pantry. Think the scheme through carefully from a practical angle. In small quarters, one area may have to fill more than one function. When this is the case, plan the room to be as flexible as possible. This can be done by using as many movable pieces as possible, making quick changes easy.

In your first plan, include everything—all furnishings, decorative objects, and elegant touches that you really want to have, after careful and practical consideration. Then classify your list, putting each item in order of importance to your general plan.

Avoid Impetuous Buying. At this point, consult your budget. If you haven't already worked one out, don't go any further until you have. Then stick with it. *Don't do any impetuous buying.* No matter how good a sale looks nor how tempting the bargains seem, no purchase will be a bargain unless it is what you need and what you will like in your home.

One young couple, who had worked out a careful plan based on their budget and had agreed exactly on how it was to be developed, encountered a high-pressure salesman. Insisting that it would be an economy to buy the best, he sold them a highly styled sofa for $1400. But perfect as it looked in the showroom, when the sofa was delivered not only did nothing they had look well with it—for this impulsive purchase did not fit into their total decorating plan—but because of the damage to their budget, they had to buy the cheapest kind of bedroom furniture. The beds were uncomfortable and they never liked the looks of the room. But they did learn a lesson, the hard way. Today, they won't buy a thing without carefully consulting their budget and considering their over-all plans.

You can benefit from their experience. Buying the best can be an economy, but if it costs $400 that isn't in your budget, it probably isn't and will simply throw off all your other plans. You

have to be sensible. Sometimes you do have a chance to buy some item that you need and plan to get eventually (but not right now) at a very special price. If this happens, sit down and see if you can adjust your budget to make the purchase possible. Modify your budget, yes—but don't blow a hole in it. It will take you a long time to recover if you do.

Plan Your Purchasing So the Effect Is Cumulative. A practical method is to put everything you want on a graded scale. Work out your budget first, then make your complete list—everything you want. Start at the top with things that seem most essential and grade down to those that are least needed. Keep your eye on the over-all idea, with a mental picture of the final results. Buy each piece with the finished room in mind. By following this method instead of the "see it and buy it" plan, you will end up with a much more satisfactory home and a minimum of expensive mistakes. Although you may get some small objects that don't quite live up to your general idea and have to be discarded, there shouldn't be any major mistakes. Don't be discouraged by an occasional change of likes and dislikes; it probably means that your taste is developing. With planned purchases you can start seeing results faster than is possible with haphazard buying, since the progress will be cumulative. And progress that you can really see will be more encouraging than all the talk in the world.

You have analyzed your space and decided what kind of activities it must provide for. You know the room and have a tentative list of furnishings and equipment necessary to fulfill the general function and create the room you want. Now, you are ready to plan a layout. In order to do this, you must draw a floor plan (instructions follow).

Usually, the furniture can be arranged in several different ways. One way is probably better than any other. On your floor plan, you can experiment and find out which arrangement seems to work best. You can also get some idea, if you use your imagination, of the way it will look. Both functionally and aesthetically, the success of your room will depend in large part on the way the furniture is arranged. Remember what you have learned about the principles of design and take plenty of time in working out your arrangement.

THE FLOOR PLAN

What Is a Floor Plan?   Architecturally, a plan view of anything is what you would see if you cut it off horizontally just above the bottom. A floor plan is an architectural scale drawing of one or more rooms, showing the arrangement and horizontal dimensions. Your floor plan will tell you the size and arrangement of rooms and give the location of all windows, doors, and other architectural features. Although an architect must also design the vertical parts of a building—a drawing of the design for each wall is called an elevation—he usually starts his designing with a floor plan of the house or apartment. When his design is completed, blueprints are made, which, with specifications, tell the contractor just how to construct each room.

For you, the floor plan is an accurate diagram on which you can arrange your furniture. On this plan, you can arrange and rearrange, to your heart's content, without the slightest danger of an aching back. On his blueprints, the architect uses certain symbols to indicate such things as electrical outlets, light switches, etc. Although these symbols will vary some with architects, on the whole they are standard and will not differ greatly from those given on the copy of the blueprint shown below. Sort out the symbols that you need so that you can use them when you are ready to read your own blueprints or to lay out a drawing of your own floor plan.

Measuring a Room.   Those of you who do not have blueprints will need to do your own measuring. It will help to keep track of the dimensions if you will draw a freehand diagram of the room and write in each measurement as you take it. For instance, to measure the room shown, draw a rough rectangle, mark each door and window and any breaks or projections of the wall, then start at the corner by the left door and measure from there. As you get a dimension, write it on the diagram in the proper place. When you have finished measuring around the room, measure the over-all length and width as well. You can check your first dimensions by totaling those on each wall: if they aren't the same as your over-all dimension, you've made a mistake someplace and you had better find it to save yourself some trouble, later.

Measure the openings of doors and windows —do not include the trim. If you want that measurement, take it separately and indicate on your diagram what it is. If you do include the trim in

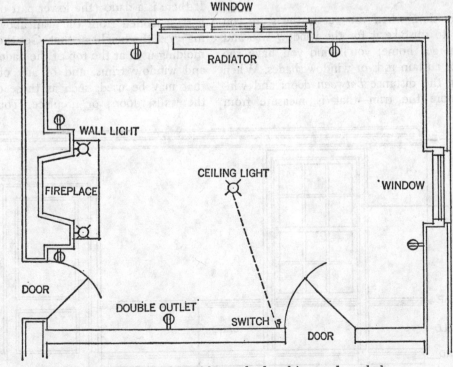

Fig. 27 A floor plan with standard architectural symbols.

opening to opening. Be sure to show the location and size of all registers or radiators or any kind of built-in equipment on your plan, whether it is on the floor or wall, or both.

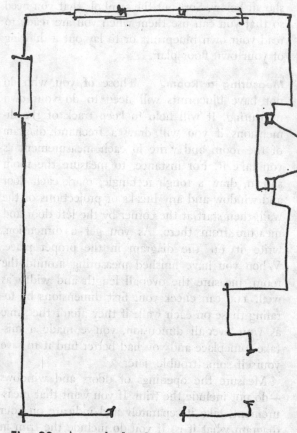

Fig. 28 A rough sketch to use when measuring.

your dimension, when you get to the store you are likely to mistake it for the window size and when you get home, you'll find you have the wrong size curtain rods or window shades. When measuring the distance *between* doors and windows, ignore the trim—that is, measure from

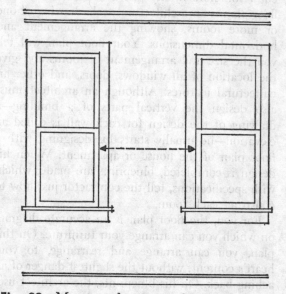

Fig. 29 Measure the space from opening to opening of doors and windows.

Measure all heights on the wall. With windows and doors, take only the openings. Get the width of any baseboard or molding next to the floor. If there is a dado (the lower part of a wall when it is separated from the wall above by a molding), get the height of that. Get the width of the molding used at the top of the dado, of the doors and window trims, and of any other moldings that may be used, such as those on panels, on the walls, doors, or fireplace. You won't need

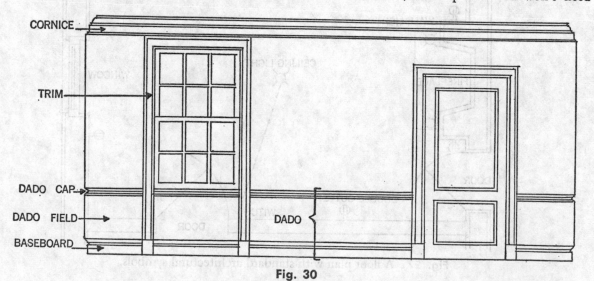

CORNICE
TRIM
DADO CAP
DADO FIELD
DADO
BASEBOARD

Fig. 30

these for your floor plan but you may need them later and it is always best to do a complete job while you are at it. Draw a rough diagram of each wall, as you did for the floor, and put your measurements on it.

Locate all electrical or other outlets, using blueprint symbols. Check with the sample blueprint to see if you have included all the kinds of information given there. If the room has structural projections, corners, or any kind of a break in a wall—and most new apartments do—be sure to show them on your plan. It can cause trouble if you buy a large piece of furniture to fit a certain space, then find it can't be used because you forgot to show exactly how the room was laid out. It has been done many times. Don't overlook anything that is actually there. If you do, you may make some serious errors in your furniture arrangement that will throw off your whole scheme in the actual room.

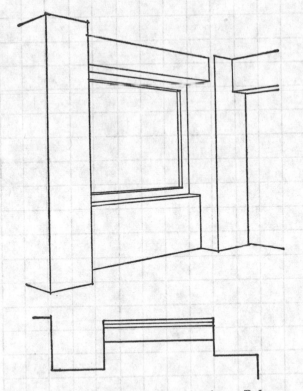

Fig. 31 *Above* structural projections. *Below* as they appear on the floor plan.

Drawing to Scale. As you can readily understand, floor plans cannot be drawn full size. To be practical, drawings must be much smaller than the room or house they represent. Since every part

of the design must bear an accurate and precise relationship to every other part, the solution is a scale drawing. All floor plans are drawn to scale. This means that a certain dimension—from 3/32 of an inch to three inches (sometimes more) represents one foot at full size. The scales of 1/8" and 1/4" to a foot are most frequently used by architects for floor plans.

Depending on the size of the subject, the scale will be large or small. A room that is eighty feet long would obviously require a very small scale, since even at a scale of 1"=1', it would take eighty inches to show eighty feet. A small room can easily be shown at a larger scale. If a room is 10'×15' and is drawn at a scale of 1/2"=1', the floor plan will measure only 5"×7½". When it is necessary to draw a piece of furniture to scale, a scale of 1½"=1', or even 3"=1', may be best, since it allows more accuracy than a smaller scale and shows the design more clearly. The floor plan on Page 29 is drawn to scale of 1/4"=1'. See if you can read all of the symbols on it.

You are ready now to start your own floor plan. Page 32 is marked off in squares to make a grid. Each of these squares measures 1/4"×1/4" and equals one square foot: so the scale is 1/4"=1'. On the pages following the grid, a plan of each commonly used piece of furniture has been blocked in at the same scale. You can draw a floor plan directly on the grid, but by fastening a piece of tracing paper over it and drawing on that, you can use the grid many times. Use a soft pencil and the outline of your room will show up clearly on the tracing paper. It is a good idea to use some kind of straight edge to make your lines steady.

The next step is to convert your room measurements into an accurate floor plan, which is quite easy once you get started. Place your measurements where they are easy to see. Now, start with the top of the left-hand wall. If, for example, it is 8' to the first door, draw a line from the upper-left corner of the grid down eight squares. If the door is 2½' wide, indicate an opening of 2½ squares. Continue in this manner all around the room. If you don't finish in exactly the same place you started, recheck your measurements all around the room and the transfer to the grid, until you do.

You may prefer to draw your floor plan at some other scale than the 1/4"=1' scale of the grid. If another scale seems more convenient, you will

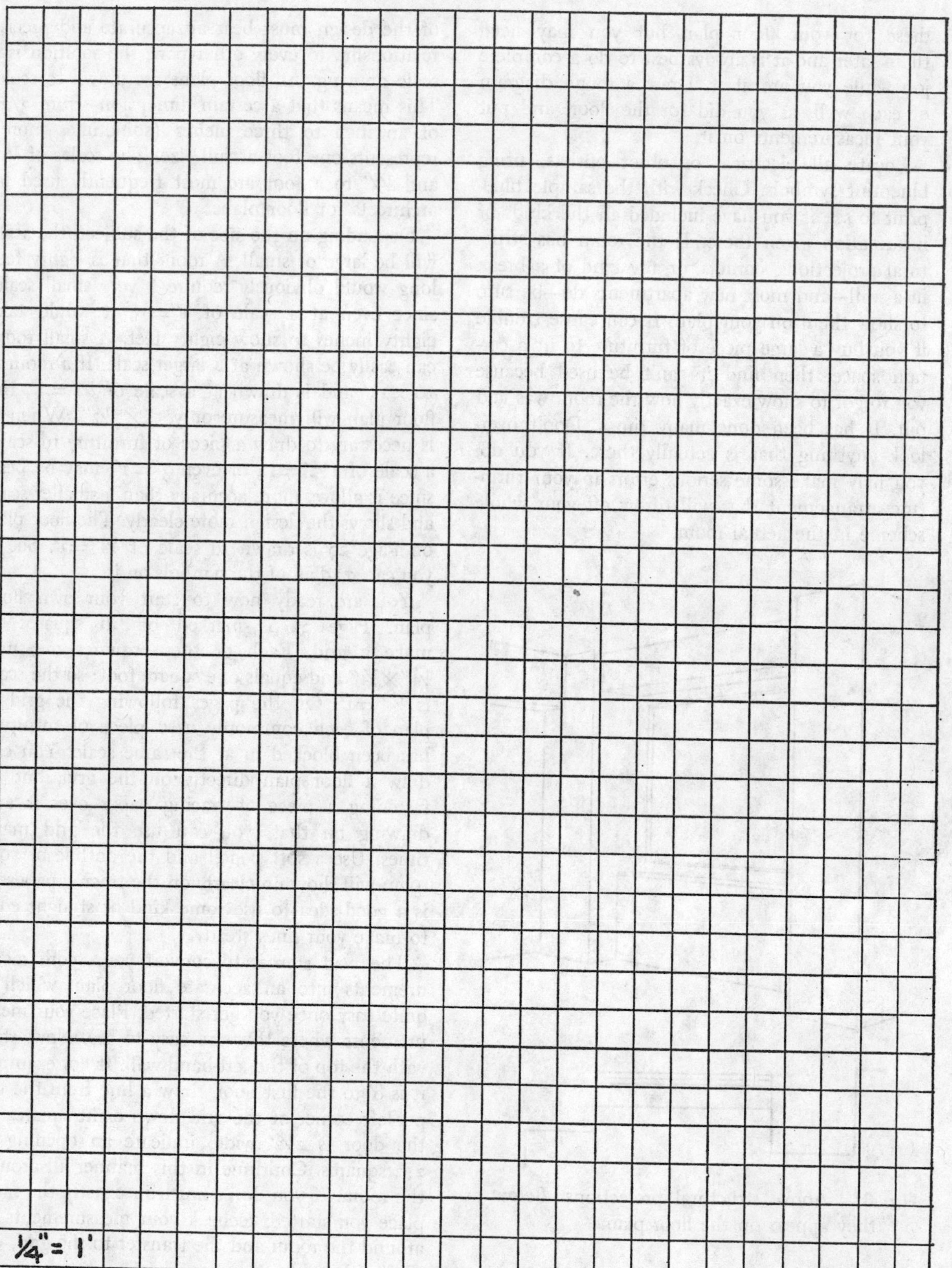

¼" = 1'

Fig. 32

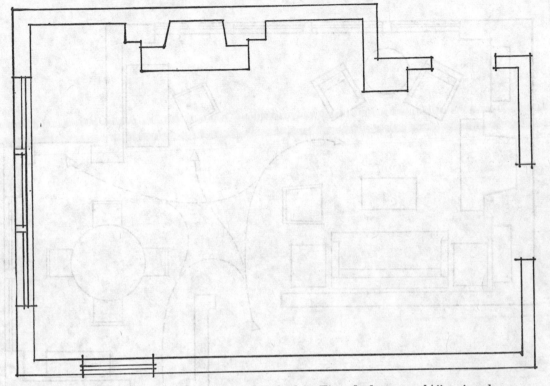

Fig. 35 A floor plan of the room sketched in Fig. 28, drawn to ¼″=1′ scale.

want a scale ruler, available at any art-supply store. (It might be a good idea to give yourself a number of lines to measure out to scale before you start to set up the floor plan.) When you block in the plan view of your furniture (similar to that in Fig. 37), be sure you use the same scale as your floor plan. It isn't easy to notice the difference, if the scales are fairly close, and many a professional has gotten badly confused trying to fit furniture cut out at a scale of ½″=1′ into a floor plan drawn at a scale of ⅜″=1′. Even if you plan to draw your own floor plan, it would be a good idea to follow instructions on the grid, first.

ARRANGING YOUR FURNITURE

Once your "room" is completed on the floor plan, you are ready to "furnish" it. You can cut out the model furniture, but by tracing, you save the models to use again. If tracing-paper furniture seems too thin to work with, transfer it by means of carbon or a soft pencil line on the wrong side, to brown wrapping paper. Cut out models only

for the furniture you have, or plan to have, in your room. If you have actual measurements of your own furniture, or sizes of what you expect to get, use them—rather than the standard sizes shown here.

Although you'll be—and should be—just as interested in appearance and beauty as use, start with function. Traffic patterns must be worked out at the beginning. Every piece of furniture should be placed to accomplish its purpose in the most effective manner. Carefully note where all openings are: doors into other rooms, halls, or closets—and windows. Consider the function of each piece of furniture that you plan to use. Arrange the furniture so it is easily accessible, yet blocks no passageways. Allow enough space in front of cabinets so they can be opened, without interfering with traffic.

Leave the way to windows sufficiently clear so they can be adjusted without straining. Have seating groups open enough to appear inviting. Don't place heavy pieces where they block any kind of function. You may have a large chair near a television set that doesn't obstruct the view, but makes tuning difficult. If you do, find someplace

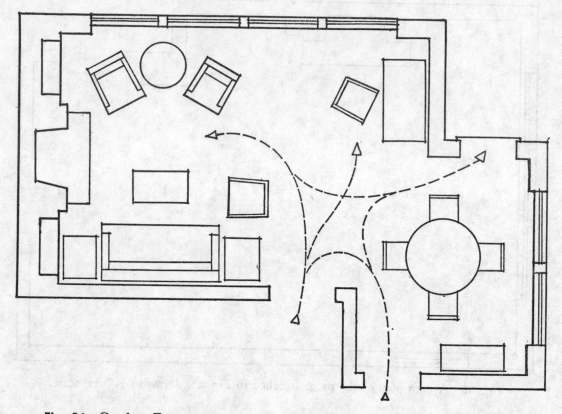

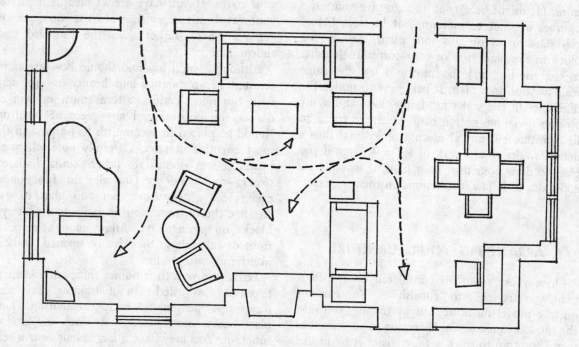

Fig. 36 Good traffic patterns. *Above* in a modern room. *Below* in a traditional room.

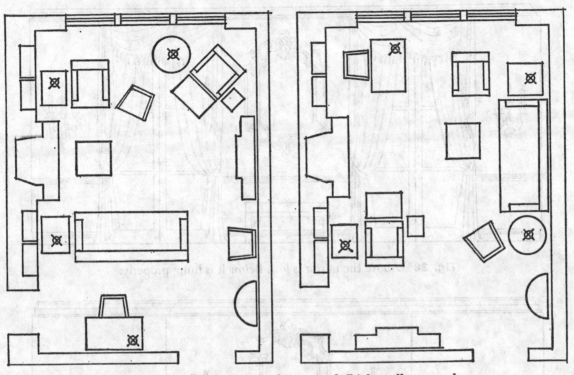

Fig. 37 *Left* furniture poorly arranged. *Right* well arranged.

else for it. Small pieces, such as light tables and stools, should be kept far enough from traffic areas so they don't endanger shins. What is needed for this first arrangement is a careful analysis of the functional requirements of the room and a common-sense answer to those needs. Your solution should result in a good, well-balanced composition.

While the floor plan is the place to start working out your furniture arrangement, it can't be conclusive, since it doesn't tell you how the furniture will look in the room. Again, you need to use common sense. Keep in mind, as you work out your arrangements, exactly the kind of piece of furniture each paper block represents. The arrangement of furniture is of primary importance and can make more difference in the success or failure of your room than any one other element except color. The more important pieces should be placed first. They must be easy to use, look their best, and placed where they will not have to compete with such architectural features as doors and windows. A large, elegant mirror, for instance, is lost when it is hung between two windows that have beautiful, colored curtains. Hanging on the wall—over a fireplace or some important piece of furniture—it can really be seen and enjoyed.

An important piece, such as a handsome secretary can be used to balance architectural features. Don't use a tall piece beside a door, but place it on the opposite wall where it can balance the door. Avoid disrupting the balance of the room by putting too much furniture in one part of the room, leaving another part empty. Even if you have to juggle the function of certain pieces to make everything work, keep the arrangement balanced. And never crowd a room. Too much furniture makes a room restless.

Place your larger and more important pieces, if possible, so they will not have to be moved. The most frequently used group should be closer to the entrance than other groups, if this can be worked out within your scheme. Don't scatter the various pieces that are used for one activity around the room. For instance, keep the records and tapes as close to the player as possible. Consider lighting in connection with the placing of each piece of furniture. Try to make as much use of daylight as possible and be sure that all areas have the right kind of artificial light.

Keep Your Standards High and Personal. To the best of your genuine understanding, maintain a high standard of taste. But beware of correctness

Fig. 38   *Above* the mirror is lost. *Below* it is hung properly.

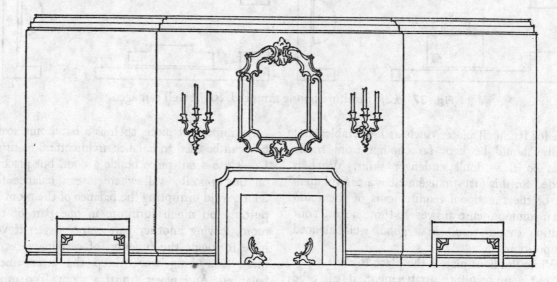

for its own sake. It usually means that you are doing something in your scheme because you think it is right and not because you understand why. Your own personality and your personal ideas and selections should be back of this plan. Don't make it self-conscious and artificial by striving for something that is insincere. Take a good look at yourself, your family, and your approach to this project—and be sensible.

Be Flexible.   Resolve to start arranging your furniture with an open mind and one aim—to achieve the most attractive and useful arrangement. Too many rooms have been doomed to failure because someone had a notion that *had* to be incorporated in the scheme. This is no place for preconceived notions. Your ideas should be

tried out, but if you find an idea unsuitable, let it go. Be sensible and reasonable, not arbitrary.

Keep It Simple.   If you can, keep your plan simple. Some people seem to feel that doing a room simply is an admission of ignorance. On the contrary, it is likely to be a sign of knowledge and confidence. Don't be afraid to keep it simple and for goodness' sake, don't try to put all of your ideas into one room. Each individual idea will be more useful and add much more if you make something of it, instead of letting it get confused with all the others.

Check the Principles and Elements in Chapter Two.   This is a good time to review the principles and elements. Many of them are essential to good furniture arrangement. Most important, you must have unity. All the pieces that you put into the room must look well together and each must be harmonious with the room. Good scale is a must: keep your furniture sizes nicely related and in tune with the room itself. Each piece must have proper proportion and a good relationship with companion pieces and the room. There should be some movement: but it must be the controlled kind that is called rhythm. The arrangement must have a feeling of balance, if the room is to be restful. Variety and contrast, properly handled, will help to emphasize the right objects and to provide the essential unity. Check each of these terms and then keep them in mind as you arrange your furniture on the floor plan.

Does Each Room Do What It Should? Everyone knows that you usually eat in a dining room, sleep in a bedroom, and cook in a kitchen. But a further look at the particular functions each room should provide may bring up some things you hadn't considered. Certainly, in many homes today, a number of functions that should be taken care of for comfortable living have been overlooked entirely.

The entrance comes first. Whether your guests walk directly into the living room, come through the garage to the kitchen, or enter through the front door into a dignified hallway, the entrance should perform its function, which is to welcome anyone who comes in. It is a transitional space, bridging the gap between the impersonal out-of-doors or apartment hallway, and the personal area that is your home. It requires good lighting, a place for coats, and a pleasant atmosphere. When it is a separate room or hall, it is also a transition from the entrance to the living part of the house. Be sure that all of your entrance areas welcome the person who enters as hospitably as the space permits.

The living room today has such a potential variety of functions that it is impossible to generalize. In order to be specific about what yours must do, go back to your list of activities that must be carried on there. Some living rooms are used for formal entertaining or as a kind of a "front," like the old-fashioned parlor in a small house or the drawing room in a larger one. Others are a gathering place for the family and are a combination library, music room, and a comfortable place to sit and chat, or read and relax. Whatever part it plays in the way you live, your living room should have a high priority and should be carefully planned, both functionally and aesthetically.

Your dining room, or whatever space is used for dining, should provide restful comfort for eating. Your bedrooms should be as quiet as possible, convenient and also restful. Any other special

Fig. 39 Hospitable entrance halls in a traditional home and a modern apartment.

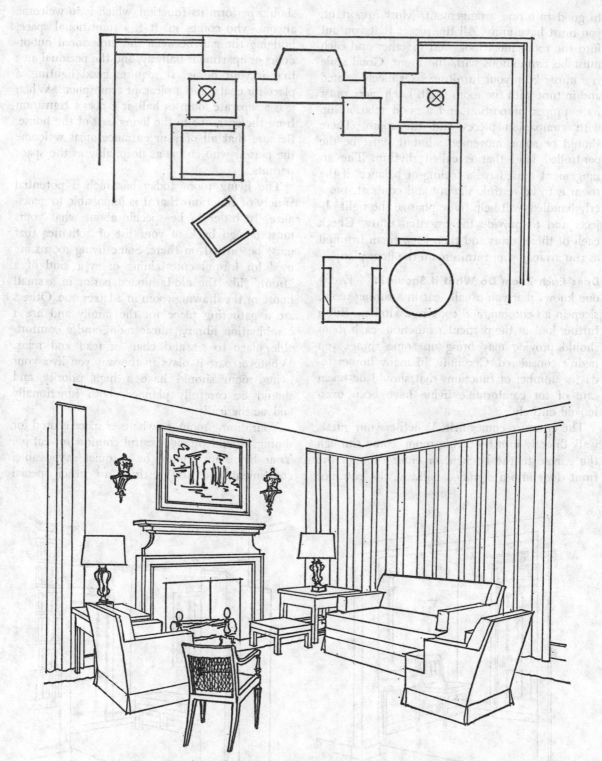

Fig. 40 A good arrangement of furniture around a fireplace.

room—library, recreation, family room—should be arranged so that it functions as efficiently as possible.

Take Advantage of Your Good Architecture. Once you have decided on your traffic patterns, you can plan to take advantage of any good architecture you may happen to have. The most natural, and one of the nicest architectural features is a fireplace. With its association of warmth and hospitality, a fireplace provides an ideal center of interest. Furniture should be arranged to make it as attractive and as useful as possible. Unless the room is very large and holds secondary groupings of importance, it is better to keep the arrangement sufficiently open so it does not seem to cut off any other part of the room.

Compensate for Bad Architecture. If the architectural detail is bad, or, as in many new buildings, practically nonexistent, your furnishings must be more interesting and more carefully planned to compensate. Bookcases with soft-colored books can be decorative, give an architectural feeling, and provide an attractive background for the dominant grouping in a room. A large window or a group of windows may also serve this purpose and, if they do, they must be made to appear important by their treatment. A painting or a wall hanging on a plain wall can do the job. But you must decide on a center of interest before you can go ahead and arrange the rest of the furniture.

Fig. 41 Bookcases and a window used as centers of interest.

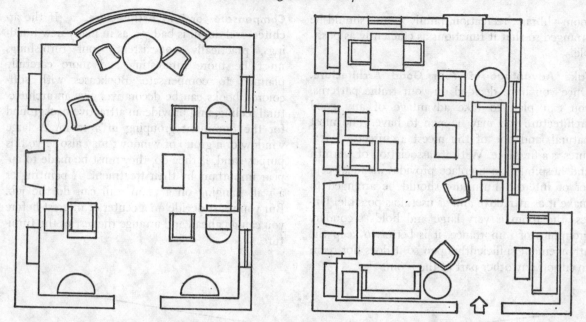

Fig. 42 *Left* formal arrangement of living-room furniture. *Right* informal.

FUNCTION—ROOM BY ROOM

Living Room.   If your living room will be used more for family living than for entertaining, arrange it with that definite purpose in mind. It should be fairly informal, with the furniture conveniently arranged. Plan the main conversation group first, and place secondary ones so they can all be opened up together. Keep different interest groups separated. The music corner, if there is one, should be as far from the reading areas as possible.

For entertaining, the arrangement should be more formal, with emphasis on conversation groups and easy movement between them. In most homes there is only one living room to serve all members of the family and guests, but other rooms may provide space for general living. For instance, if part of the family are entertaining their friends in the living room and there is a guest room not in use, it can be planned to double as a study. Here, the rest of the family can read or carry on whatever activities they like. If there is no extra space available, arrange your living room as flexibly as possible, so it will be comfortable for the family and, with a few minor adjustments, suitable for entertaining.

Dining Room.   The dining room, which may be a separate room or part of another, must com-

fortably accommodate a minimum of a table and four chairs. If there is space, you should have one or two wall pieces for storage. You will need ingenuity to make the limited spaces of so many new buildings comfortable for eating. Remember that the main function of a dining room is to provide a congenial setting for meals. Psychologists and nutritionists emphasize the importance

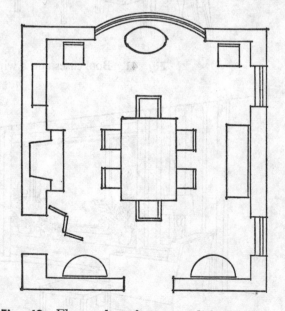

Fig. 43 Floor plan for a traditional dining room.

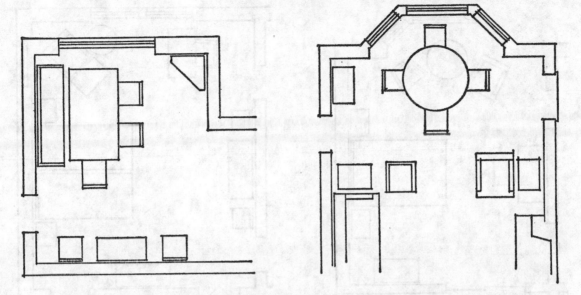

Fig. 44 *Left* floor plan of a dining room showing a banquette used with the dining-room table. *Right* an alcove in the living room used for dining.

of a peaceful atmosphere. This means that the space should be adequate, restfully furnished, and the table and chairs the right size for the people who are to use them. The arrangement should also be convenient for the person who is to do the serving.

Usually in traditional dining rooms the table is centered in the dining area and some of the chairs stand around it. Either a round, oval, square, or rectangular table can be used in this way.

In areas where space is limited, it may be better to place the long side of the table against the wall, with seating on the other side and the two ends. A bench or banquette can be built into a corner, providing seats on one side and at an end of the table. Chairs are used on the other side and at the opposite end. This utilizes all available space, but is less convenient, since one must slide into the benches and if there is more than one person, the one on the inside can't get out without someone moving. Arrangements that provide the most room may appear to be the logical answer, but always consider convenience and comfort as well as the most efficient use of space.

When you have serving or storage pieces, they should be placed where they will be easy to get at and into. A dining room almost always has some kind of a sideboard and may also have a serving table. These pieces are useful, not only for storage of silver, linen, glass, and china, but also as a

place to put things when a meal is being served. The sideboard is usually the center of interest in a dining room and the decorative pieces on it should be carefully arranged. The serving table should be placed as close to the kitchen door as possible in order to give the most convenient service. Traffic patterns in the dining room and between dining and kitchen areas are very important. Plan them carefully and you can save yourself many steps.

Bedroom. Bedrooms have two major functions—sleeping and dressing—although they are frequently used for other activities. Certain pieces of furniture are required. The minimum list includes a bed or beds, cabinet pieces for storage, mirror or mirrors, and good lighting. There should also be a comfortable place to sit.

If possible, beds should be placed where they do not face the light. And don't forget about ventilation and drafts. A bed must be made up each time it is slept in and it should either be easy to get around, or if placed against the wall, put on castors or wheels that make it simple to move. Depending on the size of the room and available wall space, twin beds can be used with a table and lamp between them; or pushed together, with lamp tables on either side. The second method is more flexible because one person can

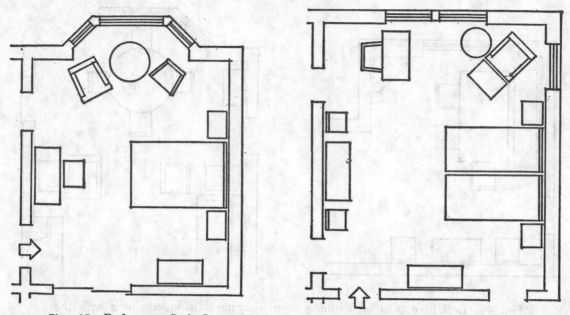

Fig. 45 Bedrooms. *Left* floor plan with a double bed. *Right* with twin beds.

keep a light on beside his bed while the person in the other bed goes to sleep in relative darkness.

Remember about traffic patterns. Try to place your bed or beds so you don't have to go around them to some piece of furniture frequently used. It can save you many steps. The way you place your bed in a small room is especially important; don't ever let it cut the room in half. Try out every possibility on the floor plan and choose the one that seems to function well and displace the least space. This will be easy to see on your floor plan. A good arrangement will definitely make more space available and the room will look larger.

Storage pieces may be built in. More often they are pieces of furniture that can be placed where you want them. Dressers and chests of drawers should be as close as possible to the closet they are used with. They should always be easily accessible, with plenty of space left in front for the drawers or doors to open. When space permits, place your dressing table where it gets good daylight. It should also be well lighted by artificial lighting. Don't use your mirrors against daylight. Try to put them where they can reflect the natural light that comes into the room. It helps to make the room brighter and also means that you can see yourself better in them.

Bedrooms are more private and personal than any other room. Usually, not more than two people share a bedroom, which means that each person can try out his personal ideas. When the bedroom is planned for one person, he can really do things his own way. It is the only room in the house where this can be done, so make the most of it.

Guest Room. A guest room needs to fulfill the requirements of a bedroom with a few extras added. A comfortable chair is needed in any guest room. There should be a convenient place for luggage—both a rack where a bag can be kept flat and easy to get into, and storage space for any other pieces. This room can be less personal than a bedroom since it will be occupied only briefly (usually) and by many different people. It is especially important to keep a guest room simple.

Child's Room. A child's room may be used for eating as well as sleeping and dressing and certainly will be used for playing. Let as much sunlight into the room as possible. The furniture should be scaled to the child and arranged to leave a clear area where he can play without bumping into anything. It is also necessary to have storage space, where the child can keep his toys, efficiently planned for his convenience.

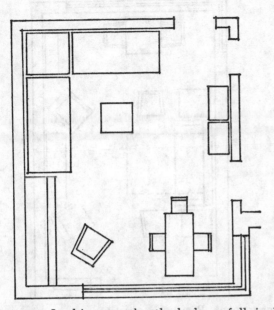

Fig. 46 In this room plan the beds are full-sized but all other furniture is scaled for children. The wall unit on the left could be a combination bookcase, desk, and storage space for toys.

Family or Recreation Room. A family room or a recreation room needs some of the same properties. Storage space is important and there

should be an adequate amount of it, easily accessible. If the room is large enough to accommodate more than one activity at a time, it should be arranged so they can be carried on with a minimum of conflict of interest. There should be well-lighted, comfortable places for reading; records or tapes should be easy to get at and handy to the player, and a convenient table, properly scaled for whatever games it is designed for, should have ample space around it. Every activity area should be well lighted. Unless the room is near the kitchen, a service pantry—with running water and, if possible, a small stove and refrigerator—is desirable. When you are doing your planning, remember to locate such a pantry in this area, if you can.

Dual-Purpose Rooms. With space at a premium today, many rooms have a double function. This is nothing new. In the homes built by the first settlers in this country, one room often had to take care of all the activities of the family. As their lives became more secure, they added rooms and gradually made their homes larger and more comfortable. But even after bedrooms were added, the kitchen and living room were often one. And today there is a trend toward kitchens that are large enough and sufficiently well equipped to take care of a number of family-living activities.

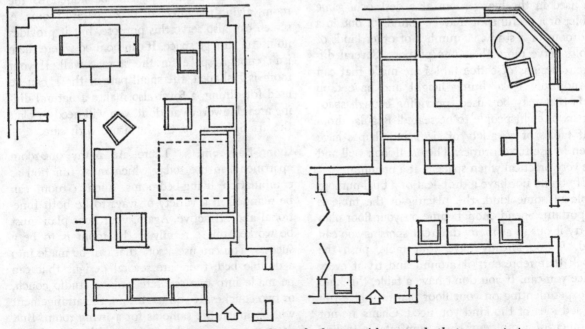

Fig. 47 *Left* a combination living-dining-bedroom with a couch that converts to a bed. *Right* another triple-purpose room, this one with a drop-leaf table.

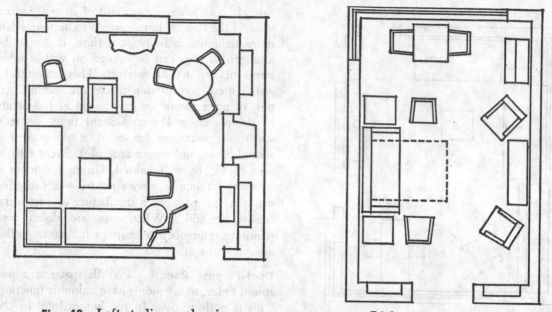

Fig. 48 *Left* studio couches in a one-room apartment. *Right* a convertible sofa.

Living-Dining Rooms. There are several common dual-purpose rooms. In many small houses and some larger ones, and in a great many apartments, part of the living room is used for dining. If you plan to do this, select your tables and chairs carefully. A console table that may be enlarged to seat ten or twelve people can be used against a wall with a chair on either side. Other chairs may be used in the living room at a desk or a game table; or a useful spot may be found for one in a bedroom or a study. A number of other kinds of tables serve more than one purpose. Several different designs of coffee tables are made that can be adjusted to a dining height and have drop leafs that may be raised, providing enough space for six or eight people to be seated. Regular drop-leaf tables of a variety of sizes and shapes have been in use for centuries. They still look well and are very practical when space is at a premium.

If you do not have a drop-leaf or a dual-purpose table of some kind, the placing of the table is important. Spend enough time on your floor plan to try it out in as many different spots as you can find. If you already have your table, push the block that represents it around and try it every place you can. If you don't have a table, this kind of experimenting on your floor plan will give you a good idea of the kind you need. Chairs are not as much of a problem, since comfortable folding chairs are available. They are practical to have,

providing you have a place to store them when not in use.

If you have enough space and want your dining area to seem to be separated from the rest of the room, a room divider, with storage space either for a radio, stereo, television, or books on the living-room side, or for china, decorative glass, or silver on the dining-room side, can be added to the room, giving the effect of two separate rooms. A screen can also serve this purpose, but it provides no useful storage space. It can be used where there isn't enough space for the storage wall. If your room is L-shaped, the small part of the L can be used for dining; a foyer also makes a natural dining area. However you do it, you will need to plan the arrangement of the furniture with care.

Living-Bedroom. There are many one-room apartments in use today which must function as combination living-bedrooms. Such a room can be planned in a variety of ways to be both functional and attractive. Again, your floor plan must be worked out carefully if the room is to be a success. You can use a sofa that can be made into a double bed; there are several designs that can be made into two separate beds, a studio couch, or two couches. If you use a sofa, the arrangement will be much the same as for a living room. But, don't use a heavy table in front of it, since it will have to be moved whenever the sofa is opened

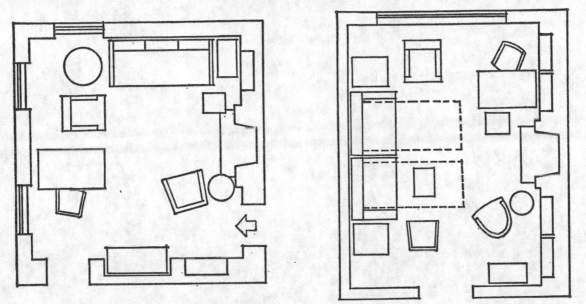

Fig. 49 Two study-guest rooms.

up and the bed made. Sofas that are comfortable when used as a single bed simplify housekeeping. Studio couches work especially well in a modern scheme and are often used against adjoining walls, with a table in the corner, to make an attractive unit. If the corner piece is a cabinet, with some convenient means of access, it provides good storage for bedding. Beds used in this way should have good castors so they can be easily moved, both for making up and for getting into the cabinet.

Study-Guest Room. The study-guest room is another frequent combination for a dual-purpose room. It seems a sensible one, since guests are not always present and study activities are rarely constant. This type of room should have drawer space, both for the owner and the guest. A good studio bed or a sofa that can be made into a bed, a convenient table and lamp and a place for luggage are all that the guest needs for his comfort. Built-in units are often found in such rooms. They provide more storage space for the owner while still leaving some empty drawers for the guest's use. In arranging the furniture, consider the function of the room, both as a study, and as a bedroom. It is for you to decide, knowing how it will be used, which function will be given preference.

Living-Guest Room. Sometimes the living room also serves as a guest bedroom. This is practical only under informal conditions as it isn't always possible for all members of the family to avoid the living room and the guest may have his privacy invaded. The arrangement can ease that situation somewhat, if the sofa that is used as a bed can be placed away from the main path through the room. Added privacy can be gained by the use of a screen. But the guest does need a table and lamp by the bed, and a place to put his luggage.

NOW YOU HAVE STARTED

If you have worked out your floor plan thoughtfully, on the basis of the principles and elements of good design, you are off to a good start in planning your room. In the over-all design of any room, there are other things to be considered— color, size and shape of each piece of furniture, importance of rugs, curtains, and accessories. But they can all be worked out better and you are certain to end up with a more successful room if you do first things first. Now that you have, you are ready to embark on the glorious adventure of color.

CHAPTER FOUR

UNDERSTANDING COLOR

GENERAL FACTS ABOUT COLOR

Color Has Tremendous Possibilities—IF You Know How to Use It. Color can do more than any other one element to make a room beautiful; it can also be very practical. Not only can color set a mood or key a room scheme, it can also make a room seem warmer or cooler, larger or smaller. It offers a wonderfully satisfying way to express your personality. It can make bad architectural features seem to fade into the wall, help a center of interest to stand out, and make an entire room appear unified. Color has quite a bag of magic tricks.

In order to get the most out of color, you must understand it. Recognizing good or bad color through your "color antenna" isn't enough. Color must be understood as well as felt. It is all around us and we take it very much for granted. But it is tricky. The laws of color are as definite and unchanging as the laws of gravity. Since the effect of one color on another is *always* based on these laws, they are predictable. If you are to make good use of color, you must know how it works.

You can probably detect around two thousand different colors. The number of combinations is virtually limitless. With so many colors to choose from, you must accumulate enough background so your choice will be a discriminating one. Color badly used is just as disastrous as it is effective when well used.

Light with Color. Light and color are inseparable. The kind of light has a definite effect on color, and any color that you plan to use in a room should be tried with the kind of light used in that room. If the room has good daylight and is also used at night, try out all colors under both kinds of light. You've heard someone say that a dress changes color in different lights. It does. Don't let this throw you off in the decorating of your home. Don't ever rely completely on the way a color looks in the store where you are selecting it. Manage to try it out where it is to be used before making any decision.

Color Theories. There are three kinds of theories on color. The physicist bases his color theory on light, which can be mechanically subdivided through a prism to produce the familiar colors of the rainbow. The psychologist bases his theory on sensations and emotional reactions caused by color. These theories are interesting and you can study them if you like. But it isn't necessary to comprehend them in order to understand how you can use color.

Artist's Theory—Yours. For your purpose, the theory of the artist, who makes his colors from pigment, is enough. The colors used in decorating are made from pigment or dyes, either of which you can use—and most important—control. The generally accepted theory about the spectrum colors is that red, yellow, and blue are called primary colors because they can not be reduced or subdivided. All other colors are made from some combination of these three primary colors.

The secondary colors are made from an equal mixture of any two of the primary colors. Orange has equal parts of red and yellow. Green is made from yellow and blue in equal proportions, and purple combines equal amounts of red and blue.

Other Theories. The physicist's theories are purely scientific. The psychologist's show that some of our emotional reactions are reflected in our speech. You have heard someone say he is "feeling blue," or have seen him in a "brown study." Everyone knows what it is to be "in the red," although the color of ink may have more to do with that state than emotions. Being "in the pink," on the other hand, is desirable and pleasant —like the color pink. Red is passionate, blue restful, and yellow cheerful. Purple is regal, gold luxurious, and gray calm and quiet. Black is the color of mourning, white of purity.

Psychologists have long been delving into human reactions to color. They don't have all the answers yet, but they have shown that generally people are happiest living with the colors they like best. If they are let alone, they will usually choose them to live with. So, for goodness' sake, don't be persuaded by some decorating fad or fine-sounding promotional literature to select for your own home some color that you don't really like.

MAKE YOUR OWN COLOR CHART

The one way to learn how to control color is by experimenting with it until you can foretell just what will happen when you combine colors. You can develop a sound understanding of the effect of colors on each other—either *mixed* together or *used next* to each other—only through experience. The first step in gaining experience is to make a color chart. Building your own chart is equivalent to learning the alphabet, which made it possible for you to put letters together into words and words into ideas. Your color chart will provide the alphabet and the words. Once you have these, you can go ahead and express your ideas in any way you like.

Equipment Needed.   The first step is to get the necessary equipment together. You will need either a box of water-color paints, or small tubes of paint. Tubes are much better than paints in a box because they are softer and therefore easier and more satisfying to use. Go to the nearest store where artists' supplies are sold and ask to see the color chart of students' water-color paints. ("Students'" paints costs less than "Artists'" paints, and are perfectly all right for your purpose.) Since all colors are made from the primary colors, you will start with them. Select the red, yellow, and

blue that seem to you to be the closest to what you consider pure colors—no blue in the red, no yellow in the blue, no red in the yellow. Remember, these are called primary colors because they can't be subdivided; none of them can contain any other color.

Any kind of paper that isn't too smooth will do to try out your colors. Sheets of paper shouldn't be too large and should be clipped onto a stiff board. You'll need a lot of them. A child's water-color tablet is easy to find and convenient to use. You will need a brush. Your brush may cost anywhere from twenty-five cents to a few dollars, depending on the quality you want. Ask the advice of the salesman. You don't need an expensive brush to make your chart, but some cheap ones are hardly worth taking home. Get two packages of blotters, and have some scissors handy. A good color chart, if you can find one, will help you to get your colors more accurately.

Primary Colors.   Now, spread out your materials and begin work. You'll use paper for your painting, but save some for your chart. Paint some yellow swatches on the first sheet of paper. You will (of course) have to mix the paint with water in order to spread it on the paper. If this lightens it too much, keep adding more paint until you get a good, strong color. If you have to add quite a lot of water, don't be afraid to use plenty of color. Make several samples of yellow, red, and blue, then select one of each that you think is best. Using a quarter or a small bottle cap as a guide, draw a circle on your best swatches and cut them out.

Follow Diagram in Laying Out Chart.   Follow the diagram (Fig. 50) in placing your swatches. To make the star, start with an equilateral triangle, allowing six inches to a side, and place one side at the bottom. Place an inverted triangle that is the same size on the first one, far enough below the top point so that all star points are equal. Put your yellow circle at the top, the red one at the lower left, and the blue one at the lower right. Don't paste them on until you have all of your colors mixed, but put a number on each space and a corresponding one on the back of each swatch, so you can remember which you chose. Sometimes, after all your colors have been made, you find a different swatch of some color that seems to have a closer relationship to the other

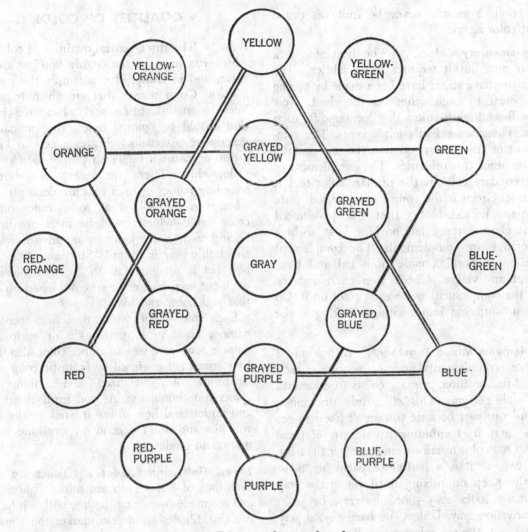

Fig. 50 Diagram for a color chart.

colors you have selected to use. But, you must make a tentative choice as you go.

Secondary Colors.   The secondary colors are made next. Mix the orange first. Theoretically, this is made from equal parts of yellow and red. However, your pigments may not be accurate enough to get the best orange from that combination, so let your eye tell—or compare it with your chart if you have one. When placed between your red and yellow, it should appear as close in color to one as to the other. Again, make several samples and choose the best one. The orange circle should be placed at the upper left of the star, midway between the yellow and red. Mix red and blue for purple, blue and yellow for green. In each case, choose your best swatch, cut out a circle,

and place your disk between its two primary colors. Now you have the six colors of the spectrum.

Half Tones.   Next, you mix the half tones that come between the adjacent spectrum colors. Yellow-orange will have more yellow than red and should be just halfway between yellow and orange in color. Red-orange will bear the same relationship to orange and red. Go right around the chart, mixing colors between those you already have: red-purple, blue-purple, blue-green, and yellow-green. Selecting the swatch that you think comes closest to being exactly halfway between any two of the spectrum colors is a challenging job and you may change your mind several times before deciding. But it certainly will sharpen your color perception. You will never be quite as casual about color again.

Complementary Colors.   The next step is a similar one, but it requires more subtlety. The colors you have so far have been made by mixing colors next to each other on the chart. Now you will work with colors that are opposite each other. These are called complements. The complement of any primary color is the one containing the other two primaries. The complement of any secondary color is the primary color that is not in it. Green is the complement of red, since it contains no red. Notice that it is opposite red on the chart. Orange has no blue in it, so blue and orange are complements. The complement of yellow is purple, made from red and blue, without any yellow. Check your chart and see what the complement is for each color on it. Do it often, until you know without looking at the chart.

Complements Mixed Together.   When mixed together, complements gray or neutralize each other. Mix the three primary colors together and you should get gray. This will require discrimination on your part because you aren't likely to get a good gray by combining equal parts of these colors. One color usually seems stronger than the other two, so it is a matter of balancing them properly. Keep on mixing until you get a gray that really looks gray—not blue-gray, or pink-gray, or yellow-gray. Unless you have a good gray on the chart, the six colors you will mix next are impossible to get. When you are satisfied with your gray, cut a disk from your swatch and place it in the center of your chart.

The last step in making your chart is to mix, for each of the six spectrum colors, a grayed tone that is halfway between the color and the gray circle in the center of the chart. Allow plenty of time to do this and don't be impatient if you have to make several tries in order to get a color that suits you. Observe carefully, each time you add any paint. See just what it does to the color you are mixing—exactly how it changes it. This kind of doing gradually becomes part of your experience, and you learn to feel it—but knowing why, not blindly. When you begin to feel this, it means that you are learning to control your colors and are well into the first step toward understanding them.

QUALITIES OF COLOR

Hue.   The three general qualities of color with which you must be thoroughly familiar are hue, value, and intensity. Hue is simply the name of a color. Color names that are given to various hues by manufacturers and advertising promotion should be ignored unless they actually are descriptive. Avocado indicates a certain kind of green, eggplant a brownish purple, parchment a yellow-white. There are dozens of interesting-sounding names of hues that are descriptive. But when you are told that some fancy-sounding color name—which could be most anything—is "being used" and when you are advised that the trend this year is toward "Startling Green," the best bet is to ignore it—to go right ahead and work out your own color schemes based on colors that you know and like.

Such color names as fawn, maize, cocoa, cinnamon, shell pink, periwinkle or seafoam—to name a few—give you a definite color idea. Don't let yourself get confused by fantastic color names or follow overgeneralized advice about what colors you should use. As you learn about color and understand how to use it, stick to the colors you like and don't depend on any kind of promotion to guide you.

Tones, Tints, and Shades.   Tones are subtle variations of hues. Tints are softer, lighter tones and are made by mixing the hue with white. Pink is a tint. Shades are deeper, darker tones and are made by mixing with dark gray or black. Navy blue is a shade.

Hues and Complements.   Every hue has its complement—the color opposite it on the chart. When complements are mixed, they neutralize each other. But, when complementary colors are used next to each other, they have the maximum of contrast. Green used next to red makes the red look its brightest. When there is so much contrast the areas should be small.

Value.   The value of a color is its lightness or darkness. The lightest value of a color may be almost white and the darkest, almost black. To make a color stronger in value, darken it. To make it weaker, lighten it. Values are very important in the proper use of color in a room. Badly used, they will destroy the unity of the room and make it restless. They should be so related that none is too conspicuous or aggressive. Each should blend with and increase the effectiveness of the others. Keep your values nicely related, so that no extreme lights or darks stand out too distinctly. If you can do this, your room can be harmonious in spite of other minor errors in design.

Intensity.   Intensity describes the strength of a color and means the amount of itself—in this case pigment—that the color contains. Intensity is the degree of brightness or dullness and differs from the value, which is the degree of lightness or darkness. Intense colors are stimulating and demand attention. To make a color more intense, add more of the pure color or pigment. To make it less intense, add white, if the paint is opaque, such as the kind you use on the wall. If it is transparent water color, add plain water. When you add white to a color to make it less intense, do so cautiously; white may do more than decrease the intensity. It sometimes changes the color, making it more delicate and slightly pastel as well as less intense.

TYPES OF COLOR SCHEMES

Related Schemes.   Schemes based on likeness are called related. Two kinds of related schemes are commonly used. One is called monochromatic and is based on two or more variations of the same hue. You can use as many variations as you like. For example, the carpet may be a deep tone of blue-green, the furniture a lighter value, the walls a soft tone, and the curtains a deeper shade. The other related harmony is called analogous. This kind of scheme makes use of variations of one primary base, for example, all hues from yellow through yellow-green toward blue, but not blue.

Complementary Schemes.   Schemes based on contrast are called complementary schemes. These schemes can become very complicated. When they do, they should be used only by experts. The two that are most frequently used are the simple complementary, based on any pair of complements, and the double complementary which includes two hues that are next to each other on the chart and their complements. In a single complementary scheme, the walls could be a soft

shade of mauve, with tones of gold in the carpet and perhaps a pattern of purples and yellows in the curtains. Purple and yellow, you will recall, are complements. The double complementary scheme includes two hues that are side by side such as blue and blue-green. Their respective complements are orange and red-orange. Walls could combine the cool tones of the blues and blue-greens, fabrics could bring in dull, orangey reds, and the carpet could emphasize either, or combine the two, which would require special care.

Both of these types of harmony require careful planning—don't ever decide on one hastily. Shades that have been softened and neutralized should be used in the larger areas. If the complements are used next to each other at full intensity, the effect will be dynamic. Don't try to do it unless your areas are carefully controlled and you feel sure that your design and the unity of the room can stand such strong contrast.

COLOR NAMES OF PIGMENTS

Colors are identified by color names. But the pigments that make the colors most commonly used have different names. The following list describes the kind of color each pigment name represents.

Alizarin Crimson—strong, pure red
Burnt Sienna—warm, reddish brown
Burnt Umber—rich, live, warm brown
Cadmium Orange—yellow-orange
Cadmium Red—yellow-red, goes toward orange
Cadmium Yellow—Deep—slightly orange
        Medium—strong, deep,
         lemon-yellow
        Light—slightly lemon
Carmine—strong red, slightly bluer than Alizarin
  Crimson
Cerulean Blue—light, sharp, peacocky blue
Charcoal Gray—dark, warm gray—almost black
Chrome Yellow—Deep—goes toward orange
        Medium—strong color, more
         lemon, less orange
        Pale—lighter, more lemon
Chromium Oxide—good, clear green, slightly yellow
Cobalt Blue—basic blue, intense sky color

Crimson Lake—strong red, between Alizarin Crimson and Carmine

Gamboge—strong, clear yellow

Geranium Lake—bright red, slightly pinker than Alizarin Crimson

Hooker's Green—good, strong green—No. 2 darker than No. 1

Indian Red—brownish or tawny red

Indigo—deep, strong blue

Lemon Yellow—color of a lemon

Light Red—lighter and more yellow than Indian Red, sometimes called English Red

Mauve—describes a variety of soft, purplish tones

Neutral Tint—deep gray with a slight purple cast

New Blue—strong, clear blue, between Cobalt and Ultramarine

Olive Green—grayed yellow-green, similar to color of a green olive

Payne's Gray—deep gray with a blue cast

Prussian Gray—sharp, strong, deep, bright blue

Raw Sienna—brownish yellow

Raw Umber—deeper and browner than Raw Sienna

Sap Green—yellow-green

Scarlet Lake—sharp, bright red—goes very slightly toward orange

Sepia—very dark, grayed brown

Ultramarine—strong, clear blue, slightly darker than Cobalt

Vandyke Brown—good, clear, strong brown

Venetian Red—yellow, tawny red, similar to Indian Red (sometimes called Turkey Red)

Vermilion—strong, clear, yellow-red, sometimes called Chinese Red

Viridian—sharp, bright blue-green

Yellow Ochre—light, slightly brownish yellow—lighter than Raw Sienna

EFFECTS OF COLOR ON A ROOM

Warm and Cool Colors. In choosing your colors, it is best to decide first what kind of a room you want. Certain colors create definite effects. The warm colors seem to come toward you and the cool colors to recede. Red is the hottest color, orange the next. The more red there is in the orange, the hotter it will be. Yellow is not as warm, but is not cool. It is the sunniest and probably the most cheerful; good to use in a dark room because it reflects the maximum amount of light. Good mixtures of reds and yellows are pleasantly cosy and informal. Darker reds and deeper golds can be used for more formal effects. Warm colors are more conspicuous than cool colors and tend to make an object or a piece of furniture look larger and more important than a cool color—especially if they are contrasted against a cool color.

Cool colors are blues and greens. They are more restful than warm ones and can be used for just the opposite effects. They make the walls recede and give a feeling of spaciousness. Interesting effects can be achieved by mixing warm and cool colors. Mixtures of blues and reds may be very gay or very dignified, depending on the values and which color predominates. If it is the red, they will be gay and may be giddy if not properly controlled. Brighter, lighter tones that go toward the pinks are often pleasant to use with soft blues. In either case, the right amount of the complementary color in the mixture will assure a soft, neutralized color. You are likely to need soft colors, when used this way, in order to avoid getting too much intensity from the sharp contrast.

Small rooms should generally be painted in the cooler colors to make the walls appear to recede. However, if you have a small, dark room and need brightness, a warm color can be used in a soft, muted tone that is light in value and low in intensity. Yellow, rather than red, is best used in mixing this color. Any kind of soft yellow-brown or a grayed chartreuse would be suitable. If you use some yellow and a little red, and keep your colors light and muted, you should be able to lighten and brighten the room, without making it look smaller.

If you should need to make a large room look smaller, this can be done by painting the walls a warm hue. The darker the hue, the more it will appear to diminish the size of the room.

Luminosity. The luminosity is also important, either where there is too much or too little light in a room. Yellow, the color that is most like the sun, has the most luminosity. Orange, which contains yellow, comes next. Green also contains yellow and can be somewhat luminous if there isn't too much blue in it. Red is hot, not luminous. Blue and purple are best used in rooms that have plenty of light.

The colors that have a light-giving potential—

those with a discernible amount of yellow in them —will be luminous. In a room where you need light, these colors can be useful. In a room that has a great deal of light—one that has a picture window facing south, for instance—luminous colors should be used cautiously. Some people like sunshine but are uncomfortable if they get too much of it. A sunny room with luminous colors can give the effect of a glare because of the combination.

Special Effects.   Many special effects can be achieved through the use of color. A long, narrow room will look wider if the end walls are brighter than the side walls. A square room will look more oblong if one or two walls are painted a darker value of the wall color. The height of the ceiling in a low room may be exaggerated by the use of strong verticals, emphasized by a contrasting color. Emphasizing panels, tall bookcases, or cabinets can help to increase the feeling of height. A light color on the ceiling will appear to make it slightly higher.

If the ceiling is too high, a wallpaper molding about three feet from the floor can be used to simulate a dado. The horizontal line this makes will help to break the height. A dark color on the ceiling will seem to bring it closer. In a room that has badly designed architectural features—unsightly beams, breaks in the wall and unattractive, decorative ornament—the defects will show less if they are painted the color of the wall. Painting the walls and ceiling one color will also contribute to the feeling of unity. Any lines in a room that disrupt or confuse the basic design should be painted the same color as the walls.

Some houses, on the other hand, have interesting architecture and really beautiful architectural detail. If you are fortunate enough to have this kind of house, you may want to feature the architecture. If you do, paint it an off-white, or a slightly lighter or darker value of the wall color. You can also use a contrasting color with good results. However, this must be done carefully and you had better wait until you understand color very well before you try.

Color should create a satisfactory aesthetic effect—do its part to make a room beautiful. This is one of the most important things it can and should do for a room. It should also provide a means for expressing the personality and tastes of the person or persons who are to live there,

and help to create the general feeling—gay, dignified, restful—that you want.

Color Areas.   The proportion of color areas in planning is very important. The largest area is the background—the floors and walls. In general, they should do what the term background suggests—stay back. A variety of wall and floor coverings being made today are not intended to stay back, but are designed to be featured. With their bold patterns and bright colors, they can be very effective. However, they are difficult to use well, so if you have a yen for them, you should probably get the help of a decorator.

Generally, it is best to use muted tones in the large areas—particularly on the walls. Again, it usually takes an expert to use the stronger ones properly. The smaller the area, the brighter the color you can use. Color intensities should usually vary inversely with the size of an area. There is no need to use bright colors at all, but if you like them, it is better to confine them to accessories, on the whole, or at least to smaller areas. But be as careful in making your color selection as you are for larger areas. A small intensely colored accessory can attract more attention in a room—and perhaps completely disrupt the unity of it—than a large sofa, covered in a soft neutral color.

Balance Your Colors.   Color is extremely important to the balance of a room. As you can see, high intensity and strong value will do one thing to a piece of furniture and the opposite kind of color will have an entirely different effect. Plan your color areas so that no one will stand out too conspicuously. One color will be dominant, but it will take its proper place in the composition of the whole. Color areas, badly put together, can ruin any room. And don't try to see how many colors you can use. Keep your color schemes simple. A simple scheme is much more likely to result in a pleasant place to live and furthermore, it will indicate that you are learning how to use color.

Suitability.   Take care to have the colors you use suitable for the rooms they are in. You know something about the effects of the different hues. Don't make a bedroom restless with a lot of bright color. Avoid bright reds or oranges for a library—or any room where people will be reading and thinking. Let your desire for strong or bright colors be expressed in a recreation or family room where there is space and activity. The fabrics used on the furniture should also be checked for suitability. Delicate tones are out of place on heavy large-scale pieces and heavy colors should not be used on dainty pieces. Use the stronger, heavier colors for the big sofa and save the delicate shades for a boudoir chair.

Historic Colors. A look at the use of color in historic design illustrates classic suitability. In each period, certain colors were used that added to the effect that the designers were trying to achieve. The large-scale, overdecorated palaces of Louis XIV used dark colors—heavy reds, greens and blues, with lots of shiny gold. When furniture became more comfortable and was scaled down to the human figure, in the period of Louis XV, colors were softer. Wood paneling was finished in wood tones or painted in off-whites or soft grays. Muted tones were used for upholstery and curtains. Golds were still used, but they were less shiny. Similar colors followed in the period of Louis XVI—perhaps even quieter ones. After the French Revolution, colors became bright again, with much use of the patriotic red, white, and blue. The Empire period had its own palette of colors—all of them strong, but not bright—grayed yellow-greens, grayed purples, dull blues, mustardy greens, and golds.

SUMMARY

In planning your color schemes, think in terms of the whole house or apartment. The larger it is, the greater variety you can use. But remember that when two rooms adjoin, you will often see the colors of both rooms together. Be sure they will harmonize. Your entire home should have unity. It isn't enough to have it in each individual room.

By now, you should know what kind of room you want and have some color samples assembled. You are ready to make a tentative choice. Unless you are feeling rested and relaxed, don't start. This is no whimsical notion. It is just good common sense. Color is very stimulating and intensely personal. It requires genuinely interested concentration. If more than one person is making decisions, there will surely be conflicting opinions that will add to the confusion. You can *not* make

sound decisions about color when you are fatigued. If you feel fresh and get off to a good start and then suddenly it seems to be an effort, it is time to stop. Don't work too long with it or try to make too many decisions at a time. You can go back to it later with fresh enthusiasm and accomplish much more.

Choose your colors on the basis of appearance, function, and your own personal tastes. Let one color be dominant in each room, with the others co-ordinated to emphasize it and to add interest. Be sure that your colors are so arranged that movement is controlled and rhythmic, not restless. Plan the over-all balance of the room, taking into consideration size, shape, and placement of each piece of furniture; pattern and texture; as well as color—thought of in terms of hue, value, and intensity. The larger areas should be kept in softer colors, the smaller ones and accents in stronger and brighter ones, if you are using them. Soft colors are easier to work with than intense ones. The brighter the color and the sharper the contrast between colors, the more knowledge you will need to use them well.

In nature, we learn to accept a general gradation of values—from light above us, middle tones in the distance close to the horizon, to stronger, deeper ones below. This is a natural arrangement and unless your colors are actually bad, if they follow this value scale, they should look well. While you are learning to use more difficult colors, stick to this formula. For example, a dark floor or rug, such as a deep green, a soft, slightly-grayed yellow-green wall, and an off-white ceiling would make a good scheme.

Always consider the function of the room first, in planning. Work closely with whatever you have selected to key your scheme and don't choose anything without referring to it. Choose the background colors first, for the floors, walls and ceiling; the secondary colors, such as curtains and larger pieces of furniture next; and your accents and accessories last.

Never try to carry a color in your head. Get a sample. If possible, take home any fabric or color you want to use and try it in the room where it will be used. Try all colors in all kinds of lighting and base your selection on the light that will be used most frequently in the room.

It is easier to match paint to a fabric or wallpaper than vice versa. When you are matching paint, insist on seeing a large sample on at least two walls, since the light will be different. The sample should be as large as possible—2′×3′. Consider the size, the exposure, and the lighting. The sample of a color of middle or dark value will appear lighter and less intense in a small area and seem stronger when it covers the walls. A very light color—just the opposite—will appear lighter when it is seen on the wall. It is very important to remember this. A large sample will help greatly in letting you see what you are getting and consequently avoiding a mistake.

Don't be impetuous or purely emotional about a color. Have a good reason for using each color. If you can't think of a reason—start over. And remember that simple schemes are often best.

CHAPTER FIVE

FLOORS AND FLOOR COVERINGS

START WITH THE FLOOR

Now that you are feeling at home with color and understand the principles of good design in arrangement, you are ready to start furnishing your room. The floor is the place to start.

Be Thorough as You Look into the Possibilities. In the past ten years the number of materials and designs available and suitable for floor coverings has increased so rapidly that it is impossible to keep up with the new products. Hard-surface flooring comes in a variety of materials, designs, and colors that would astound Marco Polo. The man-made fibers, such as rayon, nylon, and acrilan, and new manufacturing processes, have revolutionized the rug and carpet industry. And the old favorites, wool and cotton, both superb fibers, have been treated in a number of ways to give safer, better, and longer use. Materials in a wide variety of combinations and designs are limitless. This abundance increases your responsibility in making a good selection.

Basic Facts to Consider. There is absolutely no way of avoiding a floor in a room—no floor, no room. The part it will play in your decorative scheme, however, and the way it fulfills its function, depend on your selections. Do you want the warmth and the luxurious feeling of carpet? Do you prefer the cool briskness of a hard-surface floor? Will your floor be featured? If so, you must do it properly or you will make a shambles of the room's unity. If the floor is to remain part of the background, which is often the way to treat it (especially if you are not an expert), what kind of color will you use? Will there be any pattern?

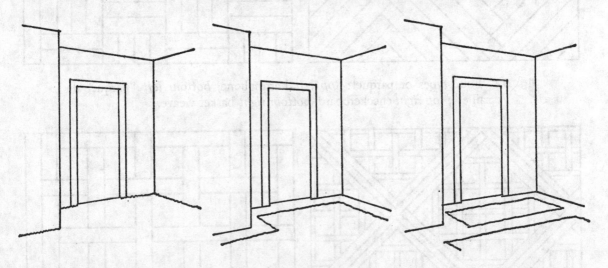

Fig. 51 Three different effects are achieved by using wall-to-wall carpeting, carpet with a margin of floor showing, area rugs.

If you decide on a carpet, do you want it installed from wall to wall? Or, do you want to use a rug with a margin of floor showing? Perhaps you want to have a beautiful floor—and also some rugs. Then you can use a few area rugs that will help to unify individual groups of furniture and at the same time will be related to the floor in such a way that they remain a harmonious part of the room as a whole.

Suppose you prefer hard-surface flooring. If this is the case, you must decide how much to feature your floor, what specific design needs the floor must fill, and then look into color possibilities. With so much to choose from, the first step is to learn all about the types of flooring available, and then see what fits best into the kind of room you want.

HARD-SURFACE FLOORING

Kinds of Hard-surface Flooring. Wood is probably the hard-surface floor you think of first and it is still the most commonly used. But marble, flagstone and slate, tile, brick and concrete

are all used inside the home more than ever before. Linoleum is the oldest of the manufactured floorings and contrary to what some people think, it is not passé at all and fulfills its function very well at less cost than most of the others. Asphalt tile, rubber tile, various kinds of vinyl tile, and cork shavings compressed into sheets are all made for use on floors.

Wood. The wood most frequently used for floors is oak. Oak wears well, is hard and durable, and looks beautiful. Pine is less expensive but is softer and more likely to wear down, and sometimes it splinters. Some pine floors wear much better than others—you must rely on your salesman for that information. Maple is hard, but not as beautiful as oak and is used in schools and shops more than in residential work. Mahogany and teak are used, but both are very expensive and are reserved for rooms when there is no budget and a special effect or great elegance is desired.

The most common kind of wood flooring is made of oak boards, from 1½" to 3" wide. The early settlers in this country used whatever they had, which often happened to be boards of odd

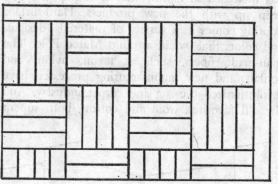

Fig. 52 Four types of parquet: *top left* herringbone; *bottom left* "parquet de Versailles"; *top right* checkerboard; *bottom right* basket weave.

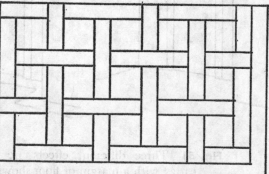

widths—some as wide as 12″, and others not more than 2″ or 3″ wide. These were held together by wooden pegs or butterfly wedges. Floors are made like this today for no reason except that someone likes the way they look.

The most decorative and finest of the wood floorings are the parquets. Parquet is a French word and refers to flooring that makes use of the strips of wood in a geometrical pattern. Checkerboard, herringbone, basket weave, and a more elaborate design called *parquet de Versailles* (found in the château at Versailles) are all used today. Checkerboard parquet is frequently used on floors in new apartment houses. The squares are smaller than those originally used and since the rooms are usually smaller, this size is more appropriate—in better scale.

Other Natural Materials and Concrete. Marble, slate, flagstone, brick, and tile are used for floors in many homes, particularly modern ones. These are all natural materials and the color selection is somewhat limited, but within their range, they can be handsome and very effective. Concrete, also used inside, can be painted, with a special paint.

Marble, slate, and flagstone are impractical for floors in a kitchen or bath unless used with small rugs (with something underneath to keep them from slipping), because they are slippery when wet. When using them in an entrance hallway, be sure there is some way of drying feet at the doorway. These materials are also hard on the feet and very cold, unless radiant heating has been installed. They are hard enough so they don't easily spot or stain. Brick and tile will show spots unless glazed.

Consider the advantages and disadvantages of each material before making a decision. Certain ones will be more practical for some kinds of use than others. If you decide to use any of them be sure to get instructions on their care when you buy them. Each requires a special kind of care and it will do a better job and look well longer if you provide that care.

Resilient Floor Coverings. There are three ways that the resilient types of floor covering can be laid. They can be used below grade, on grade, or suspended. Below grade means that they are installed partially or completely below the surrounding grade or ground level, in direct contact with the ground or with a fill which is in direct

contact with the ground. On grade means that they are laid in direct contact with the ground or with a fill which is in direct contact with the ground, but on a level with or above the surrounding grade. Suspended means above, on or below grade level with a minimum of eighteen inches of well-ventilated air space, such as a basement or well-built crawl space, below.

Asphalt Tile. Asphalt tile is the least expensive of the resilient floor coverings. It is available in a good selection of colors and designs, but unless specially treated, it is not greaseproof. It is hard and noisy and requires waxing to be maintained. It may become slippery when waxed. It can be used on grade or suspended. It usually comes in squares 9″×9″, with plain-colored feature strips 1″ wide by 36″ long. It is durable but furniture may dent or crack it.

Linoleum. Linoleum is next on the price scale. It is more resilient than asphalt tile, quieter, and will wear as well. It is made in a wide variety of colors and patterns and better grades will resist denting and cracking. It does require waxing fairly often to keep its surface but has relatively few disadvantages for its cost. When it receives the proper care, it is grease-resistant. It comes in rolls and can only be used suspended.

Vinyls. Vinyl is one of the new words in the decorating-and-design vocabulary. It is a chemical compound composed of thermoplastic resins. It has qualities that other materials do not have and is combined with these other materials to make floor and wall coverings and fabrics. It is exceptionally tough and high in tensile strength. It is not porous, so it is smoother and easier to maintain than other flooring surfaces. Clear vinyl, when combined with pigment, does not cloud colors.

Different kinds of floor covering in which vinyl is used vary according to the amount of vinyl each contains and to the manufacturing processes required to achieve the desired effect. Since pure vinyl is expensive, the higher the vinyl content, the more expensive the floor. The most expensive ones offer the finest designs and colors and the greatest durability. But, used with less expensive materials, vinyl is less costly in floor coverings and still extremely functional, with a fine selection of patterns and colors to choose from. Vinyl flooring comes in both sheet and tile forms.

Vinyl Asbestos Tile. Vinyl asbestos tile is one of the least expensive combinations of vinyl and another material. It costs about the same as linoleum and is made in a fine assortment of colors and patterns. It has exceptional durability, is easy to care for, and grease-resistant. These tiles have little resilience and are not very quiet. They can be used below grade, on grade, or suspended.

Homogenous Vinyl. Homogenous vinyl tile is a regular vinyl tile, made of vinyl resins and the most expensive tile so far described. It can be used at any level, is resistant to grease, easy to care for, and durable. It has a very hard surface and is neither quiet nor resilient. The same type of flooring is made in sheet form. Vinyl-sheet flooring can also be used at any level, has about the same degree of resilience and quietness as the tile, is more durable, less grease-resistant and equally easy to take care of.

Rubber Tile. Rubber tile is more expensive than asphalt tile, linoleum, or vinyl asbestos, but it is quieter and more resilient. A product of a natural material, it has been on the market for a long time. It is very durable, resistant to grease, and easy to care for. It is easier on the feet than some of the less resilient tiles and is often used in industrial and commercial areas. For the same reason, it is suitable for certain areas in the home. It can be had in an almost unlimited range of colors and patterns and can be used below grade, on grade, or suspended.

Cork. Cork tile costs slightly more than rubber tile. It is very quiet, resilient, and kind to the feet, but not nearly as durable as the others. It is softer and dents easily, showing marks where furniture stands or has been moved. It is likely to show grease spots and since the surface is soft, they are hard to get rid of. Cleaning and care are difficult. It cannot be used below grade, can be used on grade under certain conditions, but it is usually suspended.

Cork tile with a fused vinyl coating is the most expensive of these floorings. It looks much the same as a new, regular cork tile, but is more durable, more resistant to grease, and much simpler to take care of. It is less resilient and not as quiet as the other cork tile. It cannot be used below grade, can be used on grade under certain conditions. It is usually suspended.

Consider Function First. As you can well understand, after reading about the many qualities of resilient flooring and the variety of kinds, you

should have expert help in selecting the floor that best suits your purpose. The selection of pattern and color is wide enough so you can feel safe in finding what you want, aesthetically—*after* practical matters have been considered. Subfloor conditions, amount of moisture, traffic requirements, and maintenance costs should all be carefully evaluated before you start to make a choice of color and pattern. Be thorough. Flooring represents a large investment and you will have to live with it for a long time.

Select Color and Pattern Next. Once you have decided on the kind of floor you need, from an engineering standpoint, you are ready to choose color and design. Not only are there an incredible number of basic materials, there are an amazing number of ways to combine them. Vinyl is made to look so much like several kinds of marble, in many different colors, that you can easily enjoy the opulence of a marble floor. It is also made to simulate travertine, a unique, particularly beautiful kind of stone. These tiles can be used without any design, in a checkerboard arrangement (which gives a subtle pattern), or inlaid with metal strips or motifs such as stars, a Greek key, or circles.

Plain vinyl, black, white or colored, can be divided into diamonds, squares, or circles, or marked off in most any kind of pattern by brass inlays. Stripes of colored vinyl can be used in an area of another color, or in an allover pattern of contrasting tiles. Vinyls that look like mosaic are made in a wide range of colors. They can be used without pattern, put together in a variety of ways, or combined with plain vinyls or inlay. Other tiles simulate Delft tiles in blue or yellow on white. These are designed in a group of four—variations of a repeat—which can be used together to make a larger pattern. Some companies that make floor tiles of vinyl will match any color you want at no extra cost. A variety of simulated woods—in plain boards, herringbone, checkerboard, *parquet de Versailles* and other designs—is ready for you to use.

With such a palette of colors and diversity of designs and so many kinds of simulated materials, it should be clear that you are going to have to do some careful thinking in order to plan your floor so that it will do the job you need done and look well. The design will have a very definite ef-

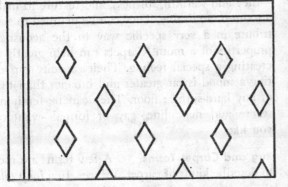

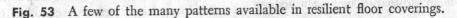

Fig. 53 A few of the many patterns available in resilient floor coverings.

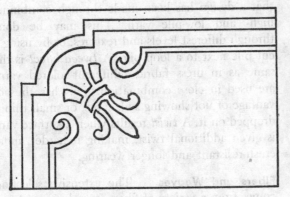

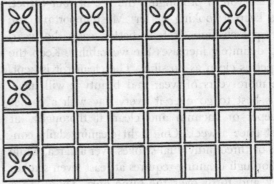

fect on the room. Is the design of the floor covering you've chosen scaled right for the room? A large, heavy pattern won't look well in a room with delicate furnishings; nor will a lot of intricate and dainty design be appropriate in a masculine room. How about proportion? If you use a border of any kind, it must seem to fit into the shape of the room.

Do the colors harmonize? Have you avoided the distraction that comes from uncontrolled movement—kept the movement in hand so it comes out as restful rhythm? Does the floor design take its place in the entire scheme, or does it threaten the importance of the center of interest? Check all principles that seem to apply to the relationship of the floor with the rest of the room. If the colors are soft, and it is to remain as background, the problem is simple. But if you want to make your floor an unusual and especially interesting one, do it carefully and be sure it is not a busy, uneasy, restless room.

SOFT FLOOR COVERINGS

While hard-surface floors are becoming increasingly popular, there are still a great many people who prefer rugs under their feet. From a design standpoint rugs or carpets can have as much and more effect as any hard-surface floor and the choice requires even more careful consideration. There is a greater variety of materials and designs to choose from. You are likely to have your rugs for some time and the investment is a substantial one, so take plenty of time to figure out what is really right for you.

The term rug is usually applied to a soft floor covering that is finished on all four sides. It may be square, oblong, circular, oval, or any kind of a freeform. Carpet, on the other hand, is woven in widths varying from twenty-seven inches to eighteen feet (if it is nine feet or wider, it is commonly called broadloom), and is usually installed more or less permanently. It can be taken up for cleaning, but that is an expensive and difficult project. It can also be cleaned, professionally, on the floor. Wherever the term rug or carpet is used in a general way, it includes all soft floor coverings.

Carpet has certain physical advantages over other floor coverings. It eliminates most of the floor noise—clicking of heels, scraping of chairs. It also acts as a blotter to absorb many airborne noises. It reduces the incidence of slipping, and if one does fall, it cushions the fall. Its pile reduces floor fatigue and it relieves coldness in areas where heating and insulation may be inadequate.

Care of Rugs or Carpets.   A few helpful hints can aid you in prolonging the life of your carpet, and keep it looking better. Most important, use a carpet cushion. It feels better, eases the wear, and definitely increases the wearability. Keep the carpet as clean as possible. The cleaner it is kept, the more years of wear and beauty it will have. It is best to go over it every day with a carpet sweeper or vacuum and clean it thoroughly at least once a week. One light cleaning daily consists of three individual strokes over an area, while a thorough cleaning requires at least seven strokes back and forth over the same area. There are a number of cleaning preparations designed especially for carpets that can be used successfully to clean the carpet in place. For a really thorough cleaning, it is best to have a professional job done—either on the floor or at a cleaning establishment, depending on the way your carpet is installed.

When carpet is installed on the stairs, it is a good idea to allow an extra foot or two. The wear is always concentrated on the edge, and if you have some extra length, the carpet can be moved before the edges show too much wear. In areas where the traffic is especially heavy, if you can occasionally either turn the carpet to change the wear patterns or rearrange the furniture, it will make the carpet last longer. Don't worry if your carpet appears to shade or shed. These are not flaws but are part of the nature of certain types of pile. Just take good care of your carpets and these apparent flaws will not bother you.

Extras Provided by Rugs and Carpets.   Rugs or carpets can do things for a room that no hard-surface floor will do. In addition to dulling noises —especially important if one lives in an apartment —they add warmth, softness, and texture to make a room more livable. They can be planned to contribute in a very specific way to the acoustical properties of a room. Carpets can help greatly in creating a special feeling. Their capacity for setting a mood is far greater and broader than that of any hard-surface floor. They can be feminine, severe and masculine, gay or formal—whatever you like.

Rug and Carpet Terms.   A few terms are used to describe kinds of carpet surfaces. In a *loop pile*, the surface consists of small loops. In a *cut pile*, the loops have been cut, exposing the ends to make a softer, richer texture. *Hi-lo texture* means that a design has been made through combining high- and low-pile yarn. This may be done through differest levels and textures, or by using a cut pile next to a loop pile. A *tweed effect* is the same as in dress fabrics—different-colored yarns are used in close combination. This has the advantage of not showing soil, spots, or small things dropped on it. A *twist* results when a surface yarn is given additional twist, making it harder, more crush-resistant and longer wearing.

Fibers and Weaves   The extensive selection comes from a variety of fibers in a choice of hand and machine-made weaves, in knotted, tufted, and tied carpets, made by hand. Until fairly recently, almost all fine rugs were made of wool. Wool is still the most widely used fiber, but today rugs are being made of wool and cotton, of synthetic fibers, and of several combinations of all of these. Wool rugs made today are better than ever before, since it is now possible to mothproof the yarn and make it soil-resistant before it goes into the rug.

Since each manufacturer can give his own trade name to a fiber, it is sometimes difficult to know what fiber is back of what name. The following table lists the manufacturers, the fiber type, and its trade name. In Chapter Eight the fibers are described.

Wool.   Since there are several important fibers used in carpets, it isn't enough to know their names. It is necessary to understand what each is and to know how it is used. Wool still rates high in every way. It comes in a wide variety of prices —only cotton is cheaper than the less expensive wool carpets. It is durable, resists abrasion, crushing, soiling, is resilient, and can be cleaned at

Manufacturer	Fiber	Trade Name
Allied Chemical Corporation	Texturized filament nylon	Caprolan ®
American Cyanamid Company	Acrylic staple	Creslan ®
American Enka Corporation	Texturized filament nylon	
	Viscose rayon staple	Enkaloft ®
American Viscose Corporation	Viscose rayon staple	Avisco ®
	Viscose rayon staple	Super-L ®
	Viscose rayon filament	Avricon ®
The Chemstrand Company	Acrylic staple	Acrilan ®
Courtaulds (Alabama) Inc.	Viscose rayon staple	Fibro ®
	Viscose rayon staple (solution dyed)	Coloray ®
	Cross-linked rayon staple	Corval ®
	Cross-linked rayon staple	Topel ®
The Dow Chemical Company	Acrylic staple	Zefran ®
E. I. du Pont de Nemours & Co.	Acrylic staple	Orlon ®
	Texturized filament nylon	Nylon 501 ®
	Nylon staple	Nylon 501 ®
Eastman Chemical Products, Inc.	Modacrylic staple	Verel ®
Firestone Synthetic Fibers Co.	Texturized filament nylon	Nyloft ®
Hercules Powder Company	Texturized filament polypropylene	Herculon ®
Union Carbide Corporation	Modacrylic staple	Dynel ®

home or by professional cleaners. There is a greater range of quality in wool than any other one fiber and the finished product varies accordingly. The finest wool carpets naturally possess the good qualities to a greater degree. You can pay anywhere from eight dollars or nine dollars a square yard to twenty-five dollars and more for a square *foot*, depending on the quality of the yarn, the kind of construction, and the cost of the design.

Cotton. The other natural fiber being used in carpets is cotton. Cotton has also been treated to give better service. The better grades wear very well, wash easily, and are shrink-resistant and colorfast. Most cotton carpets are tufted. A few are woven. Woven cotton carpets are excellent—very durable, with a one-to-three per cent shrinkproof guarantee, fast color, and fine styling.

Cotton carpets will still show soil more readily than wool and have less resiliency. They should not be permitted to get very dirty. Small rugs can be laundered in home washers and are ideal for kitchen and bathroom areas. When professional cleaning is required, have someone come to the house and examine your rug. Be sure to find out what is to be done to it and exactly what is guaranteed. The different kinds of cotton carpet and the many methods of cleaning make it important for the situation to be clearly understood.

Rayon and Acetate. Many carpets are made from rayon or acetate, two of the first man-made fibers. These are generally less expensive than wool or the other synthetics and not likely to wear quite as well. Rayon and acetate carpets vary in amount of resiliency, but on the whole have less than the other fibers. Unless treated for soil resistance, these carpets will soil easily. They can be spot-cleaned, but for general soil should be professionally cleaned and should never be permitted to get very dirty. They should not be used in areas where there is a lot of traffic. Both fibers are mothproof and mildew-resistant, but crush more easily than other fibers.

Nylon. Many carpets are made from nylon, the first of the true synthetics to become very popular. It has many advantages, and its only serious disadvantages—static and shininess—are gradually being overcome. (There is also static in wool to a lesser degree.) A spray is available for static, and a service to do the job. The service guarantees a rug to be static-free for one heating season. It must be sprayed each year. Home sprays are also available, but they aren't as effective. Too much spray causes the carpet to soil. The tendency to shininess that many people do not like—especially in certain weaves—has been reduced in the newer carpets, which are being constantly improved.

Aside from these two disadvantages, nylon is an ideal carpet fiber. It has excellent wearing qualities, is resilient, soil-resistant, and easy to clean. It can be used in any general traffic area. It is also mothproof and mildew-resistant. Nylon carpet comes in a variety of grades—although not as wide a range as wool—and, of course, the finer the grade—the more use and satisfaction it provides. Texturized nylon, which costs more than regular nylon, is the finest grade. It is exceptionally durable and has more resiliency. The texture makes it particularly resistant to soil and stains.

Acrylics.　　The newest of the synthetic fibers are the acrylics. The prices for these rugs start at about the same level as those for wool and nylon, but the best grade is much less expensive. Acrylics wear well, are resilient, resist soil, and can be easily spot-cleaned. Most of the synthetics react well to a solution of warm water and a small amount of detergent. The three best-known trade names are Acrilan, Creslan, and Orlon. Experts say that in a low-price range, you may get more for your money in an acrylic carpet than in a wool one. If you are spending $16 to $18 a square yard for carpet, your money may be better spent on wool. This is a rather general statement; of course you must check on the various qualities and have a salesman you can trust.

Woven Carpets and Rugs.　　There are three types of carpet construction in general use for machine-made carpets: woven, knitted, or tufted. The majority of carpets in the past have been woven, and weaving still accounts for a large quantity. It is important to understand the different kinds of weaves.

Wilton.　　One of the finest weaves is Wilton. Wilton carpets are woven on a loom and may be plain-colored or patterned. The name, Wilton, comes from the town in England where this kind of carpet was first made. A limited number of colors can be used in the yarns that make the surface pile. Other colors can be used in yarns not brought to the surface, providing a kind of half tone. Wilton is made in several different widths, and is closely woven, with a short, erect pile that gives it a fine texture. There are two kinds of Wiltons. The worsted Wilton is made from a longer-fibered wool that has more resilience. It is considered to be the finest kind of machine-made carpet. Regular Wiltons are also fine, but are heavier, with a coarser pile. Wiltons cost more

than the other weaves or the tufted carpets, but they look beautiful and wear well.

Brussels.　　Brussels carpets, little used today, are woven on the same kind of a loom as Wiltons, and are like the Wilton, except that the pile is left uncut. The wools used are not as consistently fine as those used in Wiltons.

Axminster.　　The Axminster is a commonly used machine-made weave. It has a very stiff all-jute back which makes it impossible to roll it crosswise: it can be rolled only lengthwise. The weave simulates handweaving, in which each knot is tied by hand. In the Axminster, each separate tuft is inserted mechanically, unlike the Wiltons. It is most frequently used for patterned and multicolored carpet—florals, oriental designs, classic, geometric, and modern motifs. There is no limit to the number of colors that can be used on a single rug.

The quality of the Axminster depends on the number of tufts in each row. If there are eleven rows to the inch, the quality is good and the rug is sure to wear well. In the higher-priced rugs where the tufts are close together, great delicacy and subtlety of design is possible. If there are fewer than five tufts to the inch, the rug will probably be inexpensive and is not likely to wear well. The price of any rug also depends on the design. If you are buying an Axminster, be sure that you are paying for the quality of the weave as well as a design that appeals to you.

Chenille.　　Chenille carpet is the most expensive machine-made carpet. As you know from chenille bedspreads, chenille is a yarn with a deep, soft pile. The name, appropriately enough, comes from the French word for caterpillar. Chenille has a deep, luxurious pile and a heavy back. It is usually made to order and can be made in any style, pattern, or shape desired, up to 30′ wide, and any length, without a seam. While it is always expensive, there is variation in quality. The depth of the pile is not necessarily the criterion; it is better to check the closeness of the weave. A low-pile chenille carpet, made with fine wools and woven closely, is a better carpet than the one with a high pile that is made from softer yarn that is loosely woven. Before you invest in any chenille carpet, find out everything about it. It will always look rich and elegant when new. Its looks ten years later will depend on factors that aren't easy to see when you are looking at the new carpet.

Velvet. Velvet is the weave used in many broadlooms and is probably used more than any other weave today. It is woven on a tapestry loom and is used most frequently for plain colors or tweeds and salt-and-pepper effects, rarely for pattern. A good velvet carpet may appear to be similar to a Wilton, but because it does not have the wool buried in the back, it is less soft and less resilient and will not wear as well. It can be made in a wide range of colors. The pile is short, with some variation in depth. If it is made from good wools and closely woven, it will wear well. However, it won't take as much heavy wear as a Wilton or an Axminster and is better used in areas where there is not a lot of traffic. It is less expensive than the other pile rugs.

Tapestry. Tapestry carpets are made like velvet carpets, but the loops are not cut, so there is no pile. Machine-made hooked rugs are usually made by this method. Other than these, few tapestry rugs are being made today. They are not resilient, nor especially soft to walk on, but they usually wear very well.

Knit Rugs and Carpets. Knitting was introduced as a method for making carpet in the early 1950s. It is like weaving in that it is done in a single operation, but unlike weaving in that the knitting process loops together the backing yarns, similar to the way it is done in hand knitting. It is used mainly for solids and tweeds. Pile can be multilevel and is more often left uncut. A few manufacturers are producing quite a large amount of knitted carpet today—other large manufacturers are making none. It has proved to be satisfactory in contract work such as hospitals, institutions, etc., and is also being used in some residential work. If it is knit closely, it will wear well. It is moderately priced.

Tufted Rugs and Carpets. In the tufting process, which came into use in the late 1940s, the piles are inserted after the backing is woven, involving two separate processes. The tufts are inserted by a machine that operates something like a sewing machine, with thousands of giant needles working at the same time. To hold the tufts in place, the rug is coated with latex and a stiff jute backing added. Although a fairly recent development, the speed and efficiency of the method has made it possible to produce good carpet at a moderate cost, and tufted carpet is being sold and used in many places where woven carpet was formerly used. A variety of textures can be made and the pile can be multilevel, cut, or uncut. It can also be made in multicolored patterns. A new process called Colorset makes it possible to print tufted carpets with no limitations on color or design. Because machines do most of the work, prices are about one third less than other woven carpets of equal quality and design.

Judging Quality. According to the American Carpet Institute, the amount of yarn that goes into a rug, more than the way it is constructed, or any other one factor, will determine the way it will wear. The theory is expressed, "the deeper, the denser, the better." The type of construction chosen should depend on the styling and the finished appearance desired, since any type of pile carpet will be good and wear well if there is enough yarn in it.

Handmade Rugs. The hand-hooked wool rugs made by several different manufacturers are usually custom-designed. They are very expensive to make, are often designed by well-known designers, and are suitable for the finest kind of room. They can be made with a raised pattern that gives a carved effect. This is done by shearing the surface on two levels, by shearing the background and leaving the pattern in unsheared loops on a slightly higher level, or by making the background shorter. Patterns may also be made by using sheared areas and unsheared loops on the same level. Patterns are used all over a rug, or as borders, often with a corner motif. Very elegant and subtle effects can be obtained in these rugs, since most of the designs are special and the work is done by hand. Wool is used more than any other fiber in these rugs.

There are many kinds of handmade rugs on the market today from all parts of the world. Indian rugs, made in our own southwest, are woven in both traditional and modern designs. Also made in this country, usually by individual craftsmen rather than large manufacturers, are the hooked, braided, and woven rugs made from yarns or scraps of wool, cotton, or silk. Depending on the style and the kind of design, these rugs can be used in a traditional or a modern room. Some of those with contemporary designs are suitable for use as area rugs in modern rooms and can supply just the dash of warmth and bright color needed.

Handmade rugs from Morocco and other countries in Africa, from several countries in Asia and Europe can be found but are not readily available. They are usually made from special kinds of wool, such as mohair, and woven on a loom in imaginative colors and interesting designs. If you feel that you would like to know more about rugs of this kind, you can get information about them through a decorator.

Oriental Rugs.   Oriental rugs have been in use since ancient times and were among the first fine rugs to be brought to this country by early settlers. From both an artistic and a material point of view, antique Oriental rugs are among the finest floor coverings ever made. For anyone who is interested in learning about them, there is a great deal of information available and there are many books on the subject (which is a very complicated one). Oriental rugs are still being made. The methods are similar to the earlier ones, but the materials and workmanship have deteriorated. The Oriental rugs most frequently used today can be classified in six groups: Persian, Indian, Turkoman, Turkish, Caucasian, and Chinese.

Persian.   Some of the finest Oriental rugs were made in Persia. The Persian rugs are covered entirely with gracefully curved designs of conventionalized foliage—vines and flowers—and some birds and animals. The pattern is definite but intricate; there is rarely a large center motif. Colors are soft and subtle, blended beautifully together. There are many different kinds of Persian rugs.

Indian.   Foliage, flowers, and animals also appear in the designs of Indian rugs. But there they are used in a natural way. They seem to be taken directly from nature, with no attempt at stylization. The colors used in the Indian rugs were much brighter and less subtle that those in the Persian rugs.

Turkoman.   Turkoman rugs are designed around geometric forms—diamonds, octagons, stars, and squares. A dark red is used more than any other one color, and browns and yellows are also favored. Turkoman rugs have a short pile, are closely woven and often have fringe.

Turkish.   The Turkish have designs that are much more carefully drawn than the others. Lines are straighter, leaves and flowers much more pointed, and the general effect is more angular. Colors are brighter, with strong contrasts. An arched prayer niche is sometimes used against a plain background as the main center motif.

Caucasian.   Caucasian rugs were made in central Asia between the Caucasian mountains and the Caspian Sea. The designs are crowded and resemble elaborate mosaics with amusing cartoonlike figures of people and animals. Caucasian rugs usually have wide borders and make use of a variety of colors.

Some fine Oriental rugs are still being made, but compared to earlier centuries, there are comparatively few. Before the beginning of the nineteenth century, rugmaking was often a family affair, and designs were passed on from father to son with great pride and care. Members of the family who did not do any weaving prepared the yarn and dyed it, and the dyers were honored above the master craftsmen who did the weaving. Since the development of interest in these rugs in the Western world and a practical means of getting them here, the demand has grown. In increasing production, materials, dyes, and workmanship have been cheapened.

European Rugs.   The very fine European rugs that are used in this country are Aubusson, Savonnerie, and needlepoint. The Aubussons are woven like tapestries, but are coarser and heavier (made in the same factory). Aubussons

Fig. 54 An Aubusson design.

are made in France and contemporary designs usually reproduce those popular in the seventeenth and eighteenth centuries, during the time of Louis XV, Louis XVI, and the Directoire and Empire periods. There is usually a center medallion, and floral, scroll, and arabesque designs. Colors are soft and subtle. Aubussons are also made by machine today.

Savonnerie rugs are hand-knotted, made with a cut pile, and a much deeper weave than the Aubusson. The designs are similar, but the rugs have a much richer look. Needlepoint rugs, made in several different countries in Europe, are not known for any special kind of design.

Fig. 55 A Savonnerie design.

Selecting Rugs. Rugs and carpets should be chosen carefully. They are a major investment and you are likely to have them for some time. If you hope to enjoy them and like them as well after several years as you did when you bought them, it is wise to make your decision on the basis of sound design principles.

Scale. If you decide to use a pattern, be sure the scale is consistent with any other pattern, and with the room. Don't use a rug with a large, heavy motif, and then upholster your chairs or paper your walls in a delicate pattern. Just as bad is a dainty rug next to a huge overscaled pattern on the walls or furniture. This doesn't mean that

everything must be the same size; but the different sizes should be pleasingly related.

Color. Color, as well as scale, will affect this relationship. If the large-scale pattern is made up of colors that are close in value, it may be all right to use it. The American Carpet Institute warns against being thrown off by fancy color names. They list seven basic color families as follows: the blues (pure blue, yellow-blue, and red-blue); the greens (pure green, yellow-green, and blue-green); the reds (pure red, yellow-red, and blue-red); the yellows (pure yellow, blue-yellow, and red-yellow); the grays (pure gray, warm gray, and cool gray); the beiges (pure beige, warm beige, and cool beige); and the browns (pure brown, yellow-brown, and red-brown).

Balance. Be careful that your rug doesn't throw your room out of balance. Too much color, too much contrast, or too much pattern will compete with the center of interest. If you are determined to feature your floor, making it the center of interest, go over every other object that you have in the room and see that the rug keeps its proper place.

Pattern. Patterns in rugs often have a great deal of movement. If the colors used are complementary, with more than a little contrast, your eye will follow the direction of the lines of the rug. Avoid too much of this kind of movement and don't use any kind of pattern that seems to make the room restless. Your rug should not only stay on the floor, it should appear to stay there. Any kind of pattern that seems to move or to come toward you is wrong.

Proportion. When a rug is used with a margin of floor showing, it makes the room seem smaller. If there is much pattern or the color of the rug contrasts strongly with the floor color, the appearance will be exaggerated: the wider the margin, the smaller the room will look. The size of the room will seem to be governed by the size of the rug, not the entire floor. This effect can be put to good use when a room is too large and you want it to appear warmer and cozier. Used in a small room, however, this kind of a rug, particularly if it has a border, can prove disastrous. If your rug and your room are both small, try to finish the floor in a color similar to the color that dominates the rug. If you like your floor as it is, or can't change it, and are getting a rug, match the floor color as closely as possible.

Fig. 56 *Above* rug with a large-scale motif incorrectly used. *Below* correctly used.

Fig. 57 *Above* a rug with a small-scale motif used improperly. *Below* used properly.

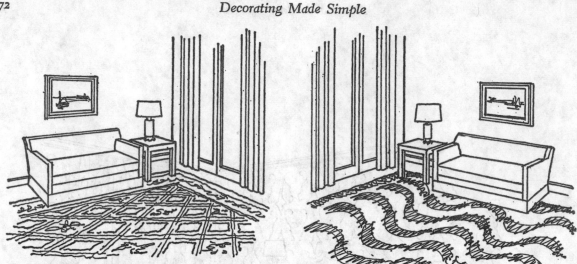

Fig. 58 *Left* a pattern that stays on the floor. *Right* a pattern that seems to come toward you.

Suitability. Whatever floor covering you choose should be suitable for the kind of room it is to be used in, both as to appearance and function. Don't put a rayon-velvet rug in a hall where traffic is heavy. Use a type of carpet that is more durable and soils less easily. The design must be in keeping with the design of the room—no Aubusson-type patterns with severe, large-scale furnishings. Your colors must also be appropriate for the kind of room, as discussed in the chapter on color. You can tell when a rug is suitable—and when it isn't. Deep-pile rugs don't belong in a room where the family carry on strenuous activities, any more than a braided rug is right in an elegant living room. Each kind of rug has a certain quality. Pick the one that seems to be right for the room you are planning.

Plain Rugs and Carpets. Plain rugs and carpets are much easier to use than those with a pattern. This may seem an obvious fact, but remember it. Some of the most beautiful rooms that have ever been designed have plain floor coverings. And you will find that you must limit your selection of everything else that goes into a room when you put pattern on the floor. Your choice of fabrics for upholstery or curtains, your use of wallpaper, even your accessories—all are not only simplified, but broader, if you have a

Fig. 59 An area rug can make a room look smaller.

Fig. 60 *Above* a strong rug pattern with fussy furniture. *Below* the same pattern well used.

plain floor. You are likely to have more fun planning a room (and probably end up with a better room) if you decide to use a plain floor covering.

If you want a room to be restful, generally speaking, a plain rug is better. It is also a good idea to have a plain floor in a small room that is slightly crowded and in any room where there is definite pattern on the wall or furniture or both. Textured and tweed rugs, and rugs with small all-over pattern give the same effect as a plain rug and don't show dirt, spots, crumbs, or dog and cat hairs as readily.

Selecting Patterns. Use care in selecting patterns. In a formal room, where there isn't much furniture and most of it is placed along the walls, a rug with a beautiful design and a central motif can be seen and enjoyed. Small-area rugs with important designs will show up well on beautiful floors where a little added interest or warmth is needed. But again, make sure the design is compatible with the rest of the room. Several small rugs of similar design and the same ground can also be used to warm or liven up a room, less dramatically. When you use small rugs, arrange them so they are consistent with the lines of the room and the group or groups of furniture they are near.

Other Practical Matters. You've seen how the

Fig. 61   A large, bold rug and area rugs used suitably.

many kinds of rugs and carpets differ in type and quality of manufacture and of design. You know that you want your rug to be suitable in all respects. In order to pick the one that will be best for you, there are a few other things to consider. You will want to check thoroughly on its wearability. Will it fade? Will the color change? How will it clean? Will it fulfill its particuar function in the room where you plan to use it? If you are starting housekeeping, remember that you will probably be adjusting your first rugs to other rooms, in larger quarters, as your family grows. If so, allow for as much flexibility as possible.

Quality. The quality of the rug, is of course, of major importance. You are familiar with some trade names, but there are many different grades made by most firms and you need to know more than the general kinds. Sometimes a medium-priced carpet will suit your purpose as well as a more expensive one, and this will allow you to replace it with something different for a later scheme. Quality can be judged on the kind of yarn used, the closeness of the weave ("the deeper, the denser, the better"), but it does take an expert to be sure about all of these facts. Given your requirements, a reliable salesman can help to select the best rug or carpet for your needs. Go to one you can trust. He is your expert.

Ask Your Salesman. The salesman can also tell you how best to take care of the particular kind of rug you get. Some rugs are much easier to care for than others. Certain weaves—those with more loops than others—may cause trouble when there is a dog in the household. The salesman can tell you all about the use of each kind of carpet. Synthetic rugs are easily cleaned, but be sure that you know exactly what kind of rug you have and the proper way to clean it.

A good salesman will also point out the fact that any light rug will darken slightly from use—dirt, not stains. Any plain-colored rug will gradually become grayer with use. This is unavoidable, but unless you realize it when you are buying and make some allowance for the change, your rug may not turn out to be quite the color you expected or wanted. Strong colors sometimes improve with a little wear, but soft colors may be ruined by wear for the effect that you wanted.

Four Decisions. There will be four decisions to make when you select a rug. If you make them in the proper order, it will help to assure your getting what you want and need. The first thing to choose is color; the second, texture or design; the third, performance; and the fourth, price. Tackle them in that order. A good salesman will find a rug in your price range that fits your color and pattern specifications. Before you start to look, sit down and organize your facts. Make a list of everything you want the rug to do for the room. List the colors in the room and get samples of as many as possible. Come to some definite conclusions about the kind of rug you want before you start. When you go to look, take your samples, the dimensions of the room, and firm ideas about what you want. You'll probably make a very good choice.

WALLS AND WALL COVERINGS

THE IMPORTANCE OF CAREFUL

PLANNING

If you have chosen the right kind of floor and your furniture is well arranged, you are ready to consider the walls. They represent by far the largest area to be decorated in a room, and they are usually there to stay. Except in a few specially designed modern houses and apartments, they are not movable. Since they take up a predominant area and can't be dismissed, it is absolutely necessary that the same principles and elements of good design that have been applied to furniture arrangement and the treatment of the floor be applied to the planning of the walls. Part of any wall is always on or near the eye level, so will always be conspicuous. It is most important to have your walls well designed.

MAKE THE MOST OF YOUR

ARCHITECTURE

Walls include openings—doors, windows, and often a fireplace. These openings, as well as any architectural features that are part of the room, such as paneling, a cornice, an intricate door or window trim, will influence your handling of the walls. If the architectural features are badly designed, you will want to overcome their effect as much as possible. If they are definitely good design, or perhaps are interesting and have character, you will probably want to include them as part of your scheme.

Paneling. Architectural wall treatment, as used in the eighteenth century in France, England, and the United States, is not seen as often now as it was earlier in this century, but there is still a fair amount of it in use. Many of the seventeenth- and eighteenth-century rooms were paneled in wood with a fireplace, and with the exception of those in the earlier provincial homes of the colonists, they were fairly formal. In the earlier part of this century much of this paneling was imported from England and France to be built into American homes, and the European styles became well known here. They were often copied and some of the reproductions were very good.

Fig. 62 A room with handsome wood paneling.

If you have a room of this kind, you should give first billing to the walls. If they are a wood tone, your scheme must be built around that. If they are painted wood or a combination of wood and plaster, you have a choice of colors. Colors for this type of walls should usually be soft and muted. The moldings that form the panels may be painted slightly lighter or darker than the rest of the walls. If this is done, the trims, baseboard, and cornice may either be the wall color or the color of the moldings.

Fireplace. Fireplaces have long since ceased to be a necessity in most homes. But they have not disappeared from the scene and probably won't, as long as people enjoy them so much. The most modern of houses is as likely to include a fireplace in its plan as any house of traditional design. Traditionally, fireplaces were used to provide heat. They still do, but except for small country cottages, summer places, and homes in warm climates where it occasionally gets a little cool, most homes depend on some other kind of heating. Fireplaces are expensive to build and, if used much, consume a large amount of fuel—which can also be expensive. But most people who have one would hate to do without it and many people who haven't one are impatiently awaiting the time when they will. A fire in a fireplace creates an atmosphere of warmth, hospitality, and pleasant sociability. There seems to be no adequate substitute for one.

A fireplace in any room has its decorative aspect. Many of them hold the spotlight as the center of interest. A well-designed fireplace makes an ideal center to feature. An ugly one should be given as little importance as possible—no emphasis at all. The kinds of design range from elegant carved wood or beautiful marble mantelpieces to contemporary ones which may be simply an opening in a rough stone wall. If you have an ugly fireplace and want to improve it, there are several things you can do.

Ugly fireplaces are usually those made of fancy brick with a great heavy shelf, built not too long after the beginning of this century; or badly designed copies of traditional mantels. If you have the first, you can improve its appearance by painting the brick the color of the wall and replacing the heavy shelf with a lighter one that is thinner with less projection. It will also help if you use a small molding between the shelf and the brick.

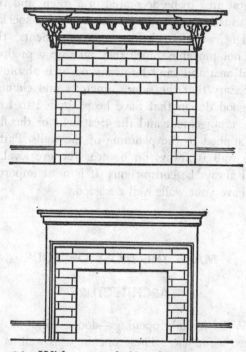

Fig. 64 With a new shelf and a coat of paint to match the walls an ugly fireplace has been made an attractive feature.

If you have a badly designed mantelpiece, it is usually possible to remove it completely. Then your wall can be plastered and a heavy molding placed around the facing. This kind of molding, called a bolection, will serve to finish off the

Fig. 63 A traditional fireplace that would certainly be the center of interest in any room.

fireplace and give it decorative importance. If there is a brick facing inside the molding, it can be painted black. If there is space for a facing, but no facing, you can cement fitted pieces of marble vinyl there and no one will ever suspect that it isn't marble.

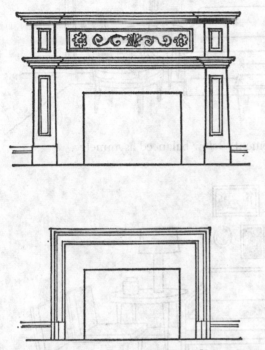

Fig. 65 Here a poorly designed traditional mantel has been replaced by a simple bolection molding.

Other Architecture. Unlike fireplaces, doors are so functional that they are rarely featured, although some may be beautiful. Your first concern will be to avoid placing furniture where it can interfere with their use. Windows are also both functional and decorative. They are so important decoratively that they will be covered in a separate chapter. Doors and doorways, built-in cupboards, cabinets, niches, and any kind of paneling must all be given careful consideration in planning your walls.

GENERAL DESIGN SUGGESTIONS

Consider Function First. In your furniture arrangement, on or near a wall, consider function first. Unless you work out the aesthetics around proper function, it won't be good design. Remember about traffic patterns and keep areas open where people will have to move about. Don't place a large piece of furniture that will be used for storage someplace where it is difficult to get to; when needed, leave space for opening doors. Place furniture to make the most of daylight and be sure that any area where artificial lighting is needed has the right kind of a supply.

Scale and Proportion. The scale and proportion of all furnishings must be right—with each other, with the wall and with the room. If you use any wall decorations such as paintings, they

Fig. 66 Furnishings in good scale and proportion. Notice that the bookcase balances the door.

Fig. 67 *Above* a symmetrical arrangement. *Below* balanced asymmetry.

must also have a proper relationship to the other furnishings. Horizontal and vertical lines should be used so there will be no restlessness—no competing between opposing lines. Don't place a tall piece of furniture near a door. A table with a tall lamp on it gives a definite vertical feeling—place it where you need it, both functionally and as part of the design.

Balance and Rhythm. Balance is especially important in composing the furnishings in relation to the walls. You can arrange them symmetrically, or you can place them so they give an illusion of balance—the optical kind. Remember that although your walls are flat, except for paintings, all of your furnishings are *three*-dimensional. You can't always place everything in such a way that perfect balance will be achieved, but you can assure a general feeling of balance.

Movement must be controlled. The relationship between straight and curved lines, properly handled, will contribute to the right rhythm. Too many curves are likely to create a restless feeling, and should be carefully balanced by straight lines in the proper place. Too many straight lines can make a room seem stiff. Balance the straight and curved lines so there are enough of both to provide a pleasing rhythm.

Color, Texture, and Pattern. Color, texture, and pattern all have a part to play. Strong color and value can be used to emphasize, soft colors to minimize, an effect. Texture on wall or upholstery will give either one more importance, because of the play of light and shadow. Pattern entirely changes the place of any piece of furniture or wall area in the design picture. Tentatively arrange your furniture to arrive at a thoughtful arrangement. If it is not satisfactory, go back and build it up again, carefully considering the application of design principles where they are needed.

Walls: Background or Basic Interest? One decision must be made about the walls at the start, in any room. Will they be treated definitely as background for the furniture? Or, will they provide an important part of the design of the room? If they are to remain as background, they will either be painted or papered in a small inconspicuous pattern. If they are to have important design interest, they may be papered, decorated with mural paintings, or finished with one of a variety of materials. They may be movable panels, free-standing units; they may be solid, grill, filigreed; they may be units of furniture containing a desk, bookshelves, drawers, and bar, storage or magazine cabinets.

PAINTED WALLS

Paint is the simplest, easiest to apply, and least expensive material for the decorating of a wall. What a coat of paint can do for a room is truly miraculous. And, walls painted an attractive color, with good paint, are practical, easy to keep clean, and decorative. The choice of paints and the selection of colors are both wide. Paint offers the quickest way of bringing background interest or color to your walls. But, unless it is chosen carefully and put on neatly, it will not do what you plan for a room. One of the main advantages of paint is that it can be mixed to match anything you choose. If you decide to have painted walls, review all the effects that colors can have on a room and select your color with great care. Then you will be ready to choose the kind of paint to use. Just as with all products, each kind of paint is more suitable for some purposes than others.

Fig. 68 Too many straight lines or too many curved lines are equally displeasing. The bottom picture shows a nice combination.

The two kinds of paint most commonly used for interiors today are oil-base paint, which is usually thinned with turpentine or benzine, and rubber-base paint, with which water is used. The degree of durability will depend on the quality of the paint. Each has its own advantages. Painters are about evenly divided on the comparative merits of oil- and rubber-base paint. If you plan to do the painting yourself, rubber-base paint may be simpler to use. It is easier to put on, dries quickly, and the odor disappears more rapidly than the odor of oil paint. It is also less messy. Hands, brushes, and anything that has paint spilled or splashed on it can be wiped off with water. Whether you use a brush or a roller or both, rubber-base paint will go on faster than oil base.

Both kinds of paint are made in flat, semigloss, and gloss (enamel) finishes. Flat paint is usually best to use on a large surface. Gloss paint is preferred for woodwork because it can be washed repeatedly. Semigloss will also take a lot of washing without looking worn. It is possible to get a dull enamel that is as durable as the more common glossy kind. It is more expensive and sometimes difficult to find, but it is very useful in a room where you do need a hard surface that will take cleaning, but do not want any shiny finishes. Washable gloss paints are usually used in bathrooms, kitchens, and often in children's and family or recreation rooms. Shiny paint reflects light, so be careful not to use it any place where it will interfere with your scheme.

Oil paints can be used on plaster, smooth cement, wood, or wallboard. Enamels can be used over any material if it has enough undercoats to make it smooth. Rubber-base paints can be used on wood, plaster, and cement, if the surface has been prepared.

Be sure of your source or brand when you buy paint. A great deal of work goes into any kind of paint job. If you do it yourself, you certainly don't want to waste your time on inferior paint. If you pay to have it done, the labor will cost more than the paint. Cheap paint is never an economy. Go to a salesman you have confidence in and listen to his recommendations for the quality of the paint. But make your own decision on the color. You know better than the salesman and you will be living there. Color is personal. If you need help, get advice from an expert and get it *in* the room where it is to be used.

When you are experimenting with color for a wall, be sure to make large samples and place them on different walls, where the light varies. One sample should be on the window wall where there is the least daylight. Another should be placed on the wall opposite the windows or on an adjacent wall, far enough from the windows so the light hits the spot. It is easier to judge the samples if you put them right up against a corner, the edge of a trim, or something solid, rather than floating against the old wall color. They should be as large as possible and a minimum of one square foot in size.

WALL COVERINGS

Wallpaper is the second most frequently used wall treatment. Like paint, it is used on any smooth surface, such as plaster or wallboard. Wallpaper can conceal defects on a plain wall more effectively than paint. For that reason it is sometimes used when a plain wall is wanted. It comes both in plain colors and in many small over-all patterns and tweed effects that give the effect of a plain color, but will further camouflage any irregularities in the wall.

Today, many other materials are pasted onto walls by the same or nearly the same methods used to hang wallpaper. Since all of these products are intended to dress the walls and contribute to the design of a room, they will be grouped together for discussion. The list includes wallpaper that is printed on rollers or hand-screened; scenic wallpaper (which was formerly hand-screened but is now also being printed on rollers); papers that are treated with vinyl; fabrics; fabrics that have been vinyl-treated; paper laminated onto cloth; papers that stick to the wall on contact (and can be peeled off); and felt.

There are a number of general advantages to be gained by using a wall covering in a room—providing you select the right one. It can help to make a room seem furnished. It provides basic design interest, and can be the strongest single element of a room scheme. When you have no architectural detail to provide interest, it can serve as a substitute. It is available in a wide variety of pattern, color, and texture, for a multitude of purposes. It hides defects in walls and can help to lessen the effect of bad architecture. It can do more to add character to a dull room than almost any other part of the design and is suitable for use in any room in the house.

Fig. 69 *Above* a room in which the walls are background for paintings and furnishings. *Below* one in which the walls are featured.

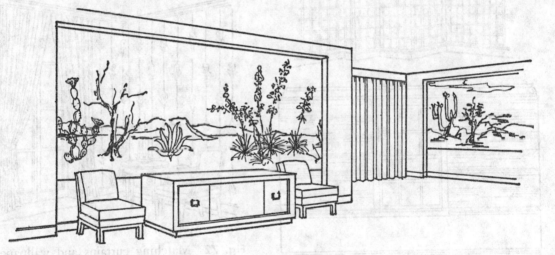

General Design Suggestions.   Consider what the different kinds of wall-covering designs can do for a room. A room that is broken up by architectural features, such as an angled roof with a dormer, or an odd-shaped room can be pulled together by means of a wallpaper or fabric. An allover geometric or floral pattern that is fairly small in scale can be hung so that the lines it makes against the ceiling or contrasting areas will be clearly seen instead of the architectural lines.

Wall coverings can change the height of a room, making it seem higher or lower, as needed. This, of course, is done by introducing a pattern with a definite vertical feeling, if the room is too low, or by using one with a horizontal feeling that seems to bring the ceiling down. The type of pattern can be chosen from a vast variety, as long as it is suitable for the room and accomplishes its mission of providing a vertical or horizontal feeling. The stripes need not be solid, they can be composed of flowers or foliage—natural or conventionalized—from a combination of geometric motifs or variations of a single one. The design must not be too busy or it will reduce the effectiveness of the lines you need.

A small room will look larger if a light-colored paper is used. It can be a small-scale design, a texture, or an embossed paper with a tone-on-tone design, as long as it is light in tone. In general, avoid a lot of pattern in a small room. Light colors are all right in a large room if you want a feeling of space, but small-scale designs are in-

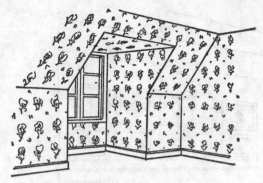

Fig. 70 Wall coverings can pull a room together.

Fig. 71 A horizontal pattern makes the ceiling seem lower, a vertical pattern makes it seem higher.

clined to lose their character when used in a large room. If you want to play up spaciousness, large-scale patterns can be very effectively used. If you prefer to make a large room look smaller and cozier, use darker colors with a fairly simple design.

Pattern can be used on the walls when there is other pattern in the room, if you plan it carefully. One of the simplest ways is to use the same pattern. Many wallpapers have matching fabrics, and some very attractive rooms have been created by using the same design for both. When this is done, be very careful of any other pattern in the room. It can be introduced, if the wall pattern is not too important; but color, scale, and general feeling must be such that the room doesn't appear restless.

Fig. 72 Matching curtains and wallpaper. Notice that the carpet and at least some of the furnishings are plain.

Pattern on walls can be tied in with some figured rugs or carpets. Color will be most important in combining these two successfully. The patterns must not be at odds with each other. If the rug is a multicolored Oriental, for example, the wall could have two or more soft colors that match tones in the rug, used in a simple design. There are few absolutes for the use of wall coverings. Sometimes most amazing things can be used together, simply by carefully applying the necessary design principles and patiently working out a precisely right color scheme.

Fig. 73 Patterned rug and wallpaper can be used effectively together if the patterns are properly chosen and the color scheme is carefully worked out.

In rooms where function is primary, such as kitchen, bath, and certain kinds of workrooms, wall coverings can be more daring, and even amusing. Furnishings in these rooms are chosen with their function as the most important consideration. They may happen to be fine design. But even if they aren't, as long as they accomplish their purpose, they must be included in the scheme. This means that the wall treatment has the pleasant responsibility of making the room attractive or interesting. In a room like this, it is possible to allow more freedom in the kind of pattern as long as you don't let color and scale get out of hand.

Always remember, when you plan the wall covering for one room, that it adjoins another. Even in a one-room house or apartment, the bathroom or kitchen facilities are part of the decorative unit. Plan adjoining rooms so they will harmonize. Otherwise, the house or apartment, as a whole, will not have unity. Without unity, it won't be a pleasant place to live.

History. The earliest wallpapers were probably made in China and were hand-painted. Some of these papers found their way to England and France in the sixteenth century. These imported, hand-decorated papers were a rare novelty, found in very few homes, at a time when the homes of many of the wealthier people had tapestry, leather, or wood on the walls. During the seventeenth century, elegant fabrics—brocades, damasks, and velvets—were favored wall coverings, and some of the early wallpapers made in France were an attempt to imitate these fabrics. A pattern similar to those used in the fabrics was printed on paper with a sticky kind of varnish, and powdered wool was scattered over it, giving it somewhat the look of soft velvet. This process was called flocking, and flocked papers are still popular today.

Jean Papillon, in France, is credited with giving the greatest impetus to the use of wallpaper, when, around the end of the seventeenth century, he planned repeating patterns that could be matched, to create a continuous design on the walls of a room. These papers were printed with blocks instead of being hand-painted and so could be produced in greater quantity. The printing of the rolls of wallpaper that we know began early in the nineteenth century.

There are many wall coverings available that reproduce the kinds of designs that were used during certain periods of history, as well as many old papers. Such papers should be properly used. If you are interested in fine papers of traditional design, you need the help of a decorator. If you

Fig. 74 A typical eighteenth-century French wallpaper.

are interested mainly in general character or feeling, a few suggestions may be helpful.

Unless you have a paneled room, backgrounds for eighteenth-century furnishings should usually be limited to wallpaper or fabrics, in designs of the period. Some are more formal than others, but none is very informal. Many of the designs were planned around a medallion, and some of them are flocked. Scenics were popular and chinoiserie was very often used. A variety of painted panels, architectural in feeling, were used. Many of them were also designed around a central motif, which was, again, often some kind of medallion, or a small scene. Arabesques, swags, ribbons, bows, shells, and a variety of ornament were used on these designs.

Fig. 75 One of a wide variety of scenics popular in the eighteenth century and later revivals.

The wallpapers of England and France differed in the same way as the furniture. The English furniture and wallpapers were as fine as the French, but not quite as elegant. In general, the rooms were consistently simpler in the English houses than in the French and the wallpapers less ornate. In this country, the wallpapers were usually copied from English papers. The early papers were very simple, and the later ones, as more wallpapers were used, were finer. Early patterns were generally small in scale—florals, geometric

designs, and stripes. The later ones are described in the preceding paragraph.

Unless you are using fine old antiques, or reproducing a room as accurately as possible, it is more important to have wallpaper that looks well than to stick close to a period paper. If your room is elegant, choose an elegant paper, such as a medallion motif, a large-scale floral, a flocked paper, or a scenic. If the room is casual or informal, regardless of period, use a paper with an informal feeling. There are many designs to choose from. Your salesman can help you to find an appropriate paper if you take along color samples and give him a description of the kind of furniture you have. If possible, get a sample to take home and try in the room.

Cleaning Wallpapers. For cleaning purposes, wallpapers fall into three categories: water-resistant, water-sensitive, and plastic. The first may be cleaned with a wet cloth or sponge and a safe washing powder, but should not be scrubbed. The water-sensitive paper should be cleaned with a commercial cleaner. Plastic papers can be scrubbed, but they won't often need to be, because they are spot-resistant. Whether they are plastic-coated or impregnated during manufacture, they will stand up under severe cleaning conditions. The price for these papers may be higher than others, but their maintenance advantages are worth the extra cost.

Vinyl Wall Coverings. In addition to wallpapers treated with vinyl, there are many vinyl wall coverings. Don't select one for your home if you tire of things quickly. If you like to change your scheme fairly often, vinyl isn't for you, because it doesn't wear out. The choice of kinds and designs produced by various manufacturers is too great to go into here. Most of them are bonded to special kinds of fabrics, and they are made to simulate many natural materials. The first vinyls were made to look like leather and the process has been so perfected that it is very difficult to tell the difference between vinyl and leather, either by looking or feeling.

The majority of vinyl wall coverings are sold for commercial or institutional buildings. But the approximately 25 per cent that are used residentially are made up of different chemical composites. They are stain- and soil-resistant; they don't crack, chip, peel, or scratch; they wipe clean with a damp cloth, and are flame-resistant in the outer layers. For your particular purpose—both as to function and design—you can find out what is available locally. You can get vinyls that simulate wood, marble, and grasscloth; and vinyls that have been teamed with fiber glass, linen, burlap, or aluminum foil—to mention a few. Once you decide what you want, from the practical angle, look for the design and color that will best suit your scheme.

OTHER WALL TREATMENTS

If you don't want a wallpaper or a vinyl wall covering, you still have a good selection for your walls. Many kinds of fabrics can be stretched and pasted or tacked on the wall. Some are made especially for that purpose, others are not. When choosing a fabric for your wall, be sure it can be hung—your salesman can tell you. Felt is one fabric that has been improved—mothproof, soil- and flame-resistant—and is available in a wide range of colors for walls. It will not shrink, and the colors are light-fast. Felt, and also a special suede-cloth wall covering can improve the acoustics of any room. The felt is also made in a filigree pattern, cut out to simulate designs in stone. It is hand washable and drip-dry.

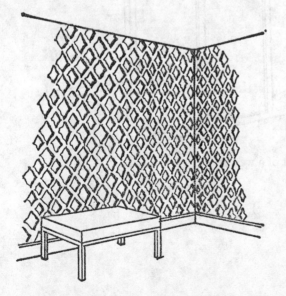

Fig. 76 Felt filigree used as a wall covering.

If you want a free-standing wall with a filigree effect, you can find many different designs. Some are made of plastic in a variety of sizes. They are structurally sound, rigid, dirt-resistant, and washable. They are prefabricated into panels and many of them can also be used for ceilings, for partial or entire walls, and for decorative screens that serve as walls. Similar panels are also available in wood in different sizes, open or with frosted fiber glass between inserts. Other intricate designs are made in iron, steel, brass, bronze, aluminum, and pewter, in several different finishes.

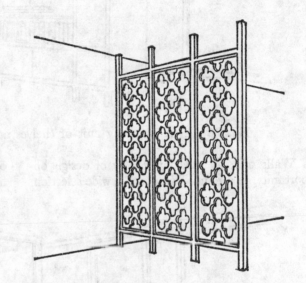

Fig. 77 A free-standing filigree wall.

If none of these ideas for walls happens to fill your needs, you may want a free-standing wall unit with a combination of cabinets and shelves. This separates two areas without providing a complete partition. It is especially useful in a room that must serve more than one purpose. The unit can contain drawers, doors, shelves, or cabinets.

A wide variety of prefabricated partitions is also available. Shoji screens, originating in Japan— light wood frames with translucent panels—have been used attractively. They can be used as a partial partition, leaving space open above or at one side. A product called curtain screen is made in combinations of wood panels with smaller sections of colored enamels put together in designs. They can be used either for interior or exterior walls.

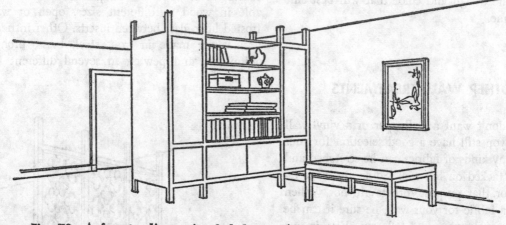

Fig. 78 A free-standing unit of shelves and cabinets makes a useful partition.

Walls offer an amazing variety of design opportunity, in a room. With such a wide selection, once again you have more responsibility for making your choice the best one for you.

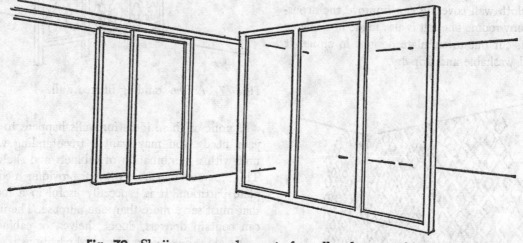
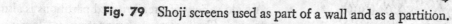

Fig. 79 Shoji screens used as part of a wall and as a partition.

CHAPTER SEVEN

WINDOWS

CHOOSE THE RIGHT WINDOW

TREATMENT

Both functionally and aesthetically, windows are one of the most important features of a room. How you treat them, decoratively speaking, will depend on your own tastes, the kind of windows you have, and the function they must fulfill in the room. In one book or article, you read that the trend is toward more elaborate treatment. In another, you are told the exact opposite. The choice, then, is up to you. Once you are familiar with the possibilities, you can choose from your favorite designs those that will be suitable for your windows.

FUNCTION, AND KINDS OF WINDOWS

Traditionally, windows had three purposes: to let in light, to permit ventilation, and to frame a view. In construction, today, one or more of these functions may not be required. Air-conditioned buildings are sometimes constructed with windows that do not open. There are buildings in which heavy opaque glass permits little light to come inside, and completely closes off any kind of a view. For most homes, however, windows are still made so they can be opened for ventilation, allow light to come through, and permit anyone inside to see whatever there is of interest that is outside.

Several different kinds of windows are used today, but they can be divided into two basic classes: fixed and movable. Fixed windows are most frequently used today as a kind of glass wall in modern houses. In older houses, decorative windows were sometimes made that could not be opened. The three most common types of movable windows are double-hung, casement, and the factory or awning type. Another kind is based on the double-hung principle, but instead of sliding up and down, the sections slide horizontally. These are often used in modern houses on one or both sides of an area of fixed windows.

Fig. 80 *From left to right:* double-hung, casement, awning, and jalousie windows.

In a *double-hung* window, the lower sash—the window frame with the glass in it—slides up in front of the upper sash, and the upper slides down behind the lower. Until comparatively recently, this type of window was used more than any other one kind in residential work and is still common. *Casement* windows are hinged at the side and swing out, or into, a room. They permit a complete opening of the space, but because of the clearance necessary for this operation, screening and curtaining may be more difficult than for a double-hung window. French windows are a variation of casements. They are used both as windows and doors in many of the houses of France.

The *awning* window is hinged at the top and swings out. Until recently, these windows were used mainly in factories and were not common in homes. Since they rarely can be opened all the way out, they don't let in as much air as a wide-open casement or double-hung window. They are so angled, when open, that they will usually keep the rain out. The *jalousie*, which looks something like a venetian blind, is based on the awning principle, with narrow strips of glass, about three inches wide, filling the opening. Windows that slide horizontally may slide into a wall or behind a fixed window, and the bottom may be a foot or more above the floor or come to the floor.

Certain architectural styles of windows also make use of either double-hung or casement windows. Dormer windows, which are set vertically into a sloping roof, may slide up and down (double-hung), or swing in or out from one side. The windows in a bay or bow window can be double-hung or casement. Often, the center section is fixed and the two side windows are movable, although some are made that do not open at all. In any of these windows, the size of the panes of glass may vary from one single pane to many small ones. The window frames are made of wood or metal.

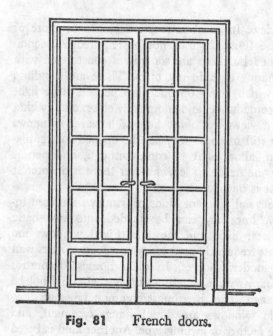

Fig. 81   French doors.

Fig. 82 *Left* dormer with casement. *Center* with double-hung windows. *Right* bay with double-hung windows.

METHODS OF CONTROLLING DAYLIGHT

Daylight in a room is desirable—but too much glaring light is not. Means of controlling daylight inside a room should be provided, both for comfort and for suitable function. The heat from the sun may also need to be screened out of a room when there is so much that it affects the temperature, making it too hot.

Roller Shades. The fixtures that hold window shades are usually set inside the trim at the top of the window. Roller shades are the most commonly used, the simplest, and the least expensive. They are made from a variety of fabrics and plastic materials. Some have designs on them: these can be made to order with a design of your own choosing. Others are made from narrow strips of wood, bamboo, or metal, in widths of ⅛" to ½", and put together with simple cords or with special ones combined with elegant yarns and tapes. All roller shades have certain disadvantages. They roll only from the top: sometimes it is better to have the top open and the bottom closed. They cut out air when they cover an open window. They are practical, however, and each type of shade had its advantages and disadvantages. Figure out your needs and likes, and decide what is best for your purpose after you have considered all of the different kinds.

Venetian Blinds. Venetian blinds are flexible, and functional in their use. Some people don't like the way they look. Others find them a nuisance to keep clean, although the new lightweight metal ones are easier to take care of than older styles. But they probably can do more to control light that any other one kind of shade and are easy to use. The slats can be angled by adjusting a cord to let in light, without sacrificing privacy. Light can be brought in from above, if it isn't too sunny, or from below, if it is. Also, if your window is close to the street or another house or building, the correct angle can give you light without permitting anyone to see in—from above or below. If your privacy is invaded from both angles, you can shut out any viewer by tilting the slats sharply, although this gives you less light. When you don't need to worry about privacy or too much light, the blind can be pulled all the way to the top and almost disappears. Fully closed, it covers the window completely. The slats can direct the light in any direction you want, making it a very practical shade.

Inside Shutters. Inside shutters, being used more and more, are also easy to adjust for varying light effects, but are hard to keep clean. If the shutter panels are not too wide, they can be hinged and easily pushed back. The louvers can also be adjusted to direct light down toward the floor, straight into the room, or up toward the ceiling. The shutters are hinged at the side and can be opened to uncover the entire window. Although they are not as easy to take care of as venetian blinds, they can, in some decorative schemes, be much more effective. They are often used in breakfast rooms, kitchens, and recreation or family rooms, but are suitable for almost any room, if they go with the general scheme. Shutters are not likely to wear out and can be counted on for years of service.

Blinds with Pulleys. Blinds that are raised and lowered by means of cord and a pulley are made from bamboo, metal, and split wood, in narrow horizontal strips, held together with tapes and adjusted by means of a cord. For a great many years, blinds similar to these have been used on porches. Today, they are frequently found inside the house. The disadvantage of these is the inclination of the pulley system to get tangled. Because of the space between the strips, these blinds often filter the light rather than provide privacy. The space also allows some air to come through. They can do a good job, within their limitations, are economical to use, and look well.

Outside Light Control. Some methods of light control are regulated by fixtures that are installed outside the window. Awnings and shutters are probably most frequently used for this purpose.

Awnings. Awnings can be very useful, though they are inclined to get hot when the sun shines on them. But they not only keep some of the heat of the sun out of the room, they make it possible to leave windows open when it rains, if there isn't too much wind. They cut off a considerable amount of light when down, but since they are usually placed where there is too much sun, this is considered desirable. They are made of a number of different materials today—fabric, wood, aluminum, and plastic. The fabrics have been improved and the selection is a very fine one—some are guaranteed colorproof for several years. Both bright and soft colors are available in an interesting collection of stripes, checks, and plaids, as well as a wonderful assortment of plain colors.

Shutters.   Shutters, installed outside the window, may be a nuisance to take care of, because of dirt and weather, but they are very functional. They direct the light by means of adjustible louvers, can be pushed back to leave a window completely uncovered, or pulled together with the louvers closed to cover it completely. Halfway between, the shutters may be closed and the louvers kept open, to direct the light and let in the desired amount of air. They are often used to protect windows, when a house that is seasonally used is closed. They look well from the outside, if they are well designed and kept neatly in order.

The variety of blinds—a combination of shutters and venetian blinds—used in Europe is worth mentioning. The designs, which are not used in this country, are both decorative and functional. Many of them must be installed during the construction of the building. Hinged at the top, and made of slats of wood or metal, many of them can also be raised and lowered from the inside by means of a heavy tape. They disappear at the top into a recessed fixture. Some are also hinged about two feet from the bottom, and have a section that can be adjusted separately, allowing air and light to come in. Some have both features; others are made with small panels within the larger ones, hinged for more flexibility. Anyone who has used some of the exterior shutters in Switzerland, Italy, Southern France, or Germany, will recall how easy they are to use and how well they do their job.

EXTERIOR APPEARANCE

Few of you will have outside shutters, but even if you do, they will be open ninety per cent of the time and you must keep in mind the appearance of the windows from the outside. Anyone living in a house with a picture window that faces a picture window across the street should feel an obligation to keep the front of his house looking as attractive as possible.

No matter how well your curtains look from inside, if you use a conspicuous pattern and leave the curtains unlined, they will not look well from the outside. In a larger house, with more space around it, it is still necessary to co-ordinate your window treatment so that whatever you use will harmonize with the exterior. Always think about how the outside will look when you are selecting curtains.

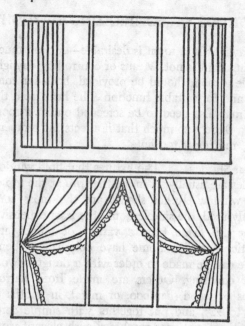

Fig. 83 *Above* a picture window with well-planned curtains seen from the outside. *Below* poorly planned curtains.

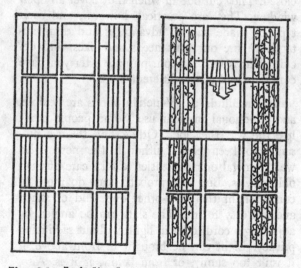

Fig. 84 *Left* lined curtains. *Right* unlined curtains, dangling swag, and the back of a valance.

CURTAINS

Why Have Curtains?   Since shades and blinds can accomplish so much, why do you want to use curtains? There are many reasons. One of the first is for your own—and your family's—pleasure. Whether you make the curtains a feature of the room or part of the background, they will be as much fun to plan as anything that goes into the room. And, in either case, they will be very important to your decorative scheme. In a rented apartment, with painted walls and a nondescript rug, you can add curtains that will relieve the monotony and give the room character and interest. They are made to size, but not permanently installed, and can be conveniently taken with you if you move.

Curtains can also help greatly in regulating the light, and will provide privacy and a good frame for a view. They can alter the apparent size or proportion of badly designed windows, appear to make the ceiling higher or lower, and cover many kinds of defects in architecture. Curtains can make a room warmer, or make it seem cooler, and can have a definite effect on the acoustics. If you think of a room that you know well when the curtains are up, and how different it looks when the curtains are down—bare and incomplete—you will realize how important curtains are in most rooms.

Curtains Defined. The terms curtains and draperies are often used interchangeably. They are not synonymous. A look at any recognized dictionary will give you the following general information. Curtains are material that has been hung to shut off, cover, hide or decorate something; a hanging that can be drawn back or up if necessary. A drapery, however, does not have these functions. It is a loosely hung, graceful arrangement of hangings, or clothing—frequently shown in painting and sculpture. An artistic arrangement of loosely hung fabric is a part of most curtains, but curtains are more than just draperies. If you want to be accurate in your terminology, call the window treatments in your home curtains, not draperies.

Kinds of Curtains. There are several different kinds of curtains. Sheer curtains that hang over the glass and rarely pull back are usually called glass or casement curtains. Heavier curtains, lined or unlined, may hang outside of the sheer curtains, or may be the only curtain at a window. In a very elegant room, there are sometimes glass curtains, a middle curtain that is drawn for privacy and to keep out the light, and heavy over cur-

tains that are purely for decoration and do not draw. The function of the first is filtering of the light and providing some privacy without closing out all the light. The middle curtains are used mainly for privacy when the lights inside are on. The third have no practical function. Today, three pairs of curtains are rarely used. Two pairs are used often, but frequently one pair does the job.

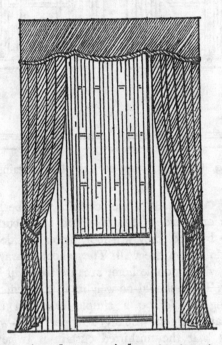

Fig. 85 An elegant window treatment using glass curtains, middle curtains, and heavy over curtains.

Each Kind to Its Function. Windows are, first of all, functional. So the primary consideration in deciding on the style that you will use is—will it work easily? It is a good idea to choose your window shade and curtains together, if you plan to use both, as one depends very much on the other. If you plan to use a sheer curtain, you have an almost bewildering choice of materials. You can have cotton, silk, linen, nylon, orlon, Saran, Dacron, Fiberglas in a variety of combinations and weaves plus fishnet and novelty weaves. Almost any color you want is also available, and there are many sheer fabrics that are woven in different color combinations or printed in stunning designs. Once you have decided on the kind of curtains you want, the next step is to see what you can get.

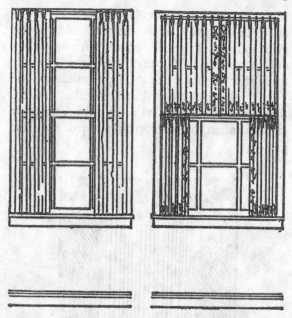

Fig. 86 Two ways to use glass curtains.

Fig. 87 Ruffled tieback curtains and sheer curtains hanging straight.

ruffled curtains that are tied back are frequently made in a sheer fabric.

Sheer Curtains.   Sheer curtains may be hung inside or outside the trim. If no other curtains are to be used, they will look better outside—on the trim or on the wall. They should always be made with a double hem, because they will hang better. There should be weights in the hem. The heading should be a simple one and allow adequate fullness—usually 100 per cent—which means that the unshirred curtain is twice the width of the window. They can hang to the sill or the floor, depending on the architecture. Unless there is a good reason for stopping them at the sill, they will look better if they hang almost to the floor—a little less than an inch above it.

Although curtains of this kind are usually hung straight, there are other ways of hanging them. They can be tied back, either with a simple band of the fabric or a cord of some kind. A distinctive mesh of linen, silk, or a synthetic fiber lends itself very well to special treatment. For example, it may be tied back at window height, or a little above, and have a valance or cornice over the top, made with an elegant swag of the material. Sheer curtains are also often made in two tiers and hung on two sets of rods. In this case, they are usually called café or cottage curtains. This arrangement provides a flexibility that is useful, since one tier can be kept open and the other closed, allowing for more control of the light. The old familiar

Casement Curtains.   Curtains for casement windows must be planned so they will not be in the way when the window is opened. If the window opens out, they should be hung inside, not on the window itself, where they would be exposed to the weather when the window was opened. On the other hand, if the window opens in, the curtains must be on the window—not the trim or frame. Otherwise the window couldn't be opened. When planning your curtains, consider every aspect of function before you take up the matter of beauty.

Heavier Curtains.   The wide variety of shapes, sizes, and arrangements of windows makes it difficult to offer any general rules for designs for heavier curtains. You must first determine what type of curtains will best fulfill your function, and then plan the specific treatment you want to use. Sometimes it is better to choose your fabric before you plan your design. If the fabric is to be an important part of the decorating scheme, this is almost certainly true.

Medium-weight Curtains—Unlined.   Generally, curtains that are not sheer should be lined. However, a number of interesting fabrics are available today that are between a sheer fabric

Fig. 88 *Left* curtains on casement windows that open in. *Right* on windows that open out.

and a heavy one in weight. They can be used to give a more definite and dramatic effect than sheer curtains, but appear lighter and airier than heavy ones. The material is made especially for curtains and is not heavy enough to be used for slip covers or upholstery. It comes in textures, small conventional patterns, larger print designs, and plain colors. The designs are not often strong enough to look unsightly from outside. The curtains should usually be made to hang to the floor and probably won't provide a dominant note in your decorating, since the light that comes through when they are unlined softens the effect of the design. They will be more important at night, under interior lighting. They can be hung and arranged in the same manner as heavier ones.

Heavy Curtains.   There is virtually no limit to the ways that heavy curtains can be arranged, nor to the kinds of fabrics and trimmings available. This doesn't mean that you should get busy and plan an elaborate arrangement. On the contrary, more often than not, in the average home, a simple one will look better. There are special places where complicated arrangements are suitable. You can decide what is best for you, after exploring the possibilities.

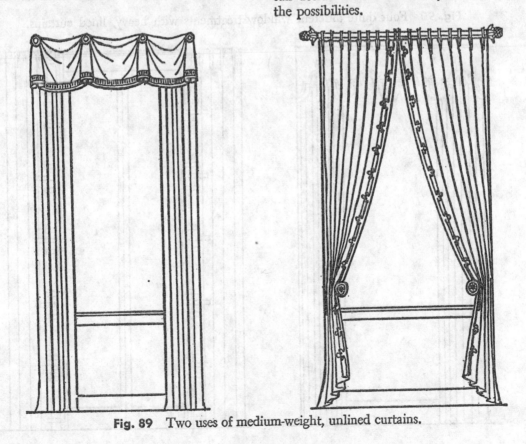

Fig. 89   Two uses of medium-weight, unlined curtains.

Fig. 90 Four quite different window treatments with heavy, lined curtains.

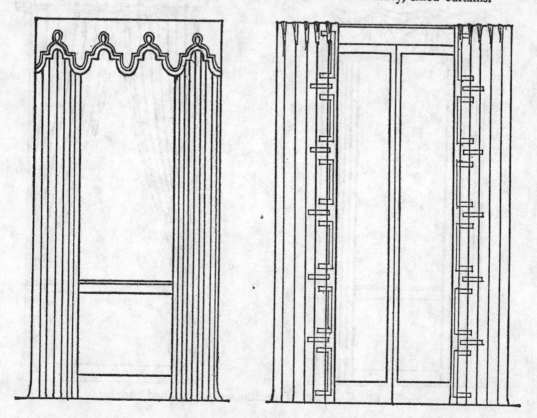

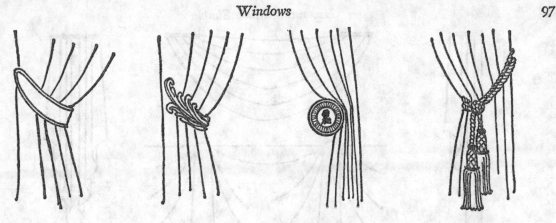

Fig. 91 A variety of tiebacks.

Many different kinds of fabrics are suitable for these curtains. There are damasks, satins, and velvets, brocatelles, brocades and taffetas, as well as many plain fabrics, a wide variety of textured ones and woven styles that combine plain and fancy ones. There are also matching fabrics—one plain or with a small allover design, the other using the same ground with a printed design on it. In planning your treatment, remember the function that must be fulfilled. The design should be suitable for the fabric and both fabric and design should suit the room.

These lined curtains can hang straight or be tied back—at a fairly high middle (just above or below, not on center) or a lower height. Refer to the Greek rule on proportion in locating your tiebacks. The way the curtains are pulled back makes a difference in the style. They can be pulled back severely, with an almost straight line along the edge, giving a tailored look; or pulled back softly, with a gentle curved line at the edge. The tiebacks can be made of the same fabric, made from a wide assortment of cords and braids, or may be metal, wood, crystal, or mirror. Study some of the arrangements illustrated for ideas. Then figure out the arrangement that would look best in your room and be most practical for your purpose.

Cornice or Valance. If you plan to use a cornice or valance, your next step is to work out a design for that. The terms valance and cornice are difficult to distinguish between because they are used interchangeably by some decorators, others make a definite distinction between the two, while still others make a *different* distinction. So, when someone speaks of a cornice or valance, be sure that you know exactly what he means.

Literally, a valance is a short drapery over the

Fig. 92 Several valances: *top* wood covered with fabric; *bottom* draped fabric.

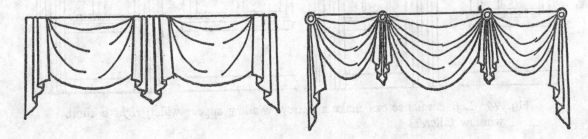

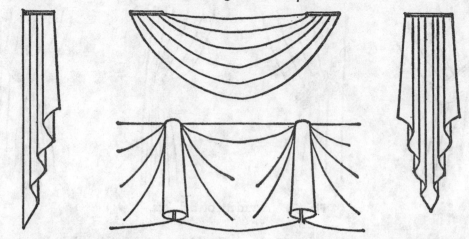

Fig. 93 Decorations for a valance: *top center* a swag. *Bottom center* swag with cartridge pleats. *Left and right* jabots.

top of a window, and a cornice is an ornamental band for covering a curtain rod. Usually, as curtains are made today, a valance is a horizontal form, either wood, or a frame of wood covered with fabric, that is used at the top of a window or above it. A cornice is used very much the same way, and either one will conceal any curtain rods used under them. In architecture, a cornice has a crown molding that projects at the top. It might be said that a valance is flat, while a cornice has a trim that projects at the top. This draws a fine line and since there is actually so little difference in the two, the important thing is to know just what you mean, and understand what the person means who is making your cornice—or valance—for you.

There are many ways of decorating a valance or cornice—with swags, various kinds of folds, pleats, jabots, and with braids, fringes, and other kinds of trims. They can also be perfectly plain and still be effective. Sometimes one fabric is used for the curtains and another for the valance. Other times the valance is made of carved or painted wood or metal.

Either a valance or cornice can be very useful in correcting defects in height, width, or proportion of windows. Either one can also help, with curtains, to pull together windows that seem too far apart. A valance above a short window gives

Fig. 94 *Left* a valance can make a narrow window appear wider; *right* a short window taller.

the effect of more height. If a window is too narrow, the valance can be extended beyond the trim on each side and the curtains hung on the wall so they cover only the edge of the window. If a window is too tall for its width and space doesn't permit the installation of the curtains on the wall, the valance can be placed inside and below the trim, cutting down the height.

Windows that are side by side, but a little far apart, or those on two sides of a corner, can be pulled together by using a single valance over all. Unless they are too far apart, the space between them can be covered by straight curtains, giving the impression of a single unit. Windows of different sizes can sometimes be equalized with the help of a valance. When one is lower than the other, the valance can be placed above the lower one and inside the trim of the higher one to make them look the same height.

Tailoring of Curtains Important.   The way your curtains are made is important. Unless you are very handy with your sewing machine and can make tailored things that really fit, you should have professional help. The finest material, made into a curtain of the most beautiful design, will not look right unless it hangs perfectly. Heavy curtains should always be lined. Sateen is traditionally the most common lining material, but in recent years, Milium has become popular. It is an insulation and is used on a number of different materials that vary in price. It comes in a grade that is similar to sateen both in price and appearance. It is very practical to use when the curtains are drawn; it keeps out heat in the summer and cold in the winter.

Some curtains should be interlined. If you are using an elegant material and want the finished curtain to look beautiful and to hang perfectly, interlining is indicated. Lining will make curtains last longer, reduces fading, and cuts out light. Sometimes the lining of a curtain is part of the design and is turned back so it can be seen. The finest curtains are sometimes lined with satin or taffeta. When you are selecting your material, hold it up and see how much sun comes through it before making a decision.

Headings.   A heading is the portion of the curtain that stands above the rod when the curtain is hung. Whether or not it shows, it will affect the way the curtain hangs. There are several different arrangements of headings. The simplest is plain shirring, which is best suited to sheer fabrics. Shirring means to gather or draw up cloth on parallel threads. Sometimes the gathering up is partly done on the rod. Simple, sheer curtains are shirred as they are pushed together on a rod that is shorter than the width of the curtains. For slightly heavier curtains, shirring is made by sewing down close but irregular gathers of material and sewing rings on the outside of the material to be slipped over the rod.

French Heading.   The French heading, probably the most commonly used, is made by gathering the material, with some kind of a stiff sizing inside, into three small pleats of equal size, pinching them together and sewing them about three to four inches from the top. The folds are spaced about six inches apart and the size of the pleats depends on how much fullness you want it to hold. The fabric falls from the pleats and the folds follow down the length of the curtain, gradually becoming less firm.

Box Pleats.   Box pleating is often used in skirts and is made the same way when used in curtains. After deciding how much fullness you want in each pleat, the material is taken in at the back, with buckram or some stiff material inside, and sewed, and then the front is pressed flat. In this type, the pleats are closer together. The space between is usually about the same width as the pleat. Since these are flat, they are often used under a valance or cornice.

Cartridge Pleats.   Cartridge pleats hold in less material. They are made by pinching in and

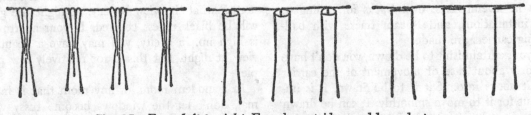

Fig. 95 *From left to right*: French, cartridge, and box pleats.

stitching down about one and a half inches of fabric, approximately three or four inches below the top. The heading is stiffened so the pleats form a kind of cartridge-shaped roll. They are smaller in scale than the other pleats. Hooks are pinned or sewed to the back of the curtains at the bottom—of any kind of a heading—and hooked into the fixtures in the rods.

Trimmings.   The number of different kinds of trimmings available seems almost as great as the variety of fabrics. There are certain basic kinds of fringes: plain fringe, tasseled, looped—any of which may be straight or scalloped—several kinds of ball fringes, and many that are much more complicated, combining two or more basic types. There are also many kinds of braids and gimps, and a fringe may be used with a braid or gimp. Trimmings may be simple, or very elegant, and are made from different kinds of materials. Very fine fringes may cost as much as forty dollars for a single yard.

A welting is a simple trim that is frequently used. It is made by covering a heavy cording with fabric. Usually a welt of the same material is best when used on curtains, but sometimes a contrasting welt is more effective. A heavy cording that is ½" in diameter when covered makes a more important finish than the more commonly used ¼" size. A double welt, two of the smaller size used together, makes a very nicely tailored trim. Trimmings may be beguiling and it is easy to let yourself get carried away by them. Remember that they should be used only if they add to the general design idea, not if they compete with it or confuse it in any way.

Fixtures.   There are a number of different kinds of curtain rods, and fixtures for each kind. Some are installed inside the window trim, some outside, on the wall, and others on the ceiling. You will have to find out what kinds of fixtures are available to you locally, and select the ones best suited to your purpose. There are round rods, ranging in diameter from ¼" to 2". Flat rods come in several sizes; oval tracks for ceiling or wall installations, and I-beam tracks with ball-bearing carriers are made.

If your curtain isn't to be drawn, you don't have to worry about ease of movement of the carrier that it hooks into. If it is to be drawn, it is important for it to move smoothly. It can be drawn by hand, or by an attached mechanism called a traverse rod. This kind of rod operates by means of a pulley, with cords at one end, which can pull the curtains together or separate them. These rods are also made to draw a single curtain across the window, either from the left or the right. Some curtains are hand drawn on rods that are meant to be seen as part of the design, in which case, decorative rings are used.

Whether or not you use a traverse rod depends on your needs. The cords can get tangled, making it impossible to move them, which is annoying and inconvenient. On the other hand, if the curtain is pulled manually, the side where it is handled will get soiled unless you are very careful. A cord, attached to the heading, or a baton to push the heading with, can help to avoid the soiling. But where children, who don't bother with the cord, or can't reach the heading with the baton, may be pulling a curtain with soiled hands, a traverse rod is probably more practical. In this age of automation, there is a fixture that is operated by electricity. To open or close your curtains with this, it is necessary only to push a button.

When buying fixtures, be sure you know exactly what kind of curtain you have. Is it light or heavy? Does it require a strong fixture? Where will it be hung? Will it draw? Rods may be purchased in regular or heavy-duty weight. Be sure there are enough carriers for the hooks that are on the back of the curtain, so they will be close enough together to hold the curtain properly when it is closed. They should not be more than three or four inches apart if the curtains are to hang right.

SUMMARY

Remember when you plan your window treatment what your window is for, and be sure that you don't interfere with its function. If you have a nice view, let it be seen. And remember that, no matter what the view by day, at night the glass will be black unless covered. If your apartment is high up, in a city, you may have a beautiful view at night. But this is for relatively few people.

In a modern room, or any room that is informal, don't let the windows become fussy with treatment. They must harmonize with the room in every way. If there is pattern in the curtains, it should be in scale with the room and everything in it. If your curtains are being featured, try to make them beautiful—and just important enough. If they are to be background, don't let them get too busy. Don't let them interfere with the room's unity. Be sure they are made properly and installed so they hang well. If you do all of these things, you will surely have curtains that do their job and look well at the same time.

CHAPTER EIGHT

FABRICS

Although the words *fabrics* and *textiles* are often used interchangeably, they are not synonymous. Fabric is any cloth, no matter how it is made. A textile is a woven fabric. Fabrics, then, are among the most important and pleasing ingredients of interior decorating. You can have the time of your life selecting, combining, and enjoying them. That is, you will if you make your selection on the basis of some sound knowledge about what will be the right kind of fabric—for both function and appearance—for your particular purpose.

KINDS OF FABRICS

There are four basic kinds of fabrics: woven, knit, felted, and tufted. In decorating, woven fabrics, or textiles, are used more than all of the others together. The process of weaving interlaces two systems of yarn at right angles to each other. The threads that go across are called weft, or filling; the lengthwise threads, warp. Knitting is the process of producing cloth with one or more yarns moving in the same direction. Felted fabrics are made by interlocking fibers by chemical action, moisture, or heat. With the exception of chenille, as used for bedspreads, there are no tufted decorating fabrics. The tufting process is used mainly in making rugs.

WOVEN FABRICS

Since the majority of fabrics used for decorating are woven, some facts about woven fabrics and the different weaves may be helpful. Weaving goes back to antiquity and the principle has changed little since the first woven materials were made; only the tools are different. Today, instead of simple handlooms, there are such incredibly complicated machines that the average person couldn't possibly understand how they work—even with a loom in front of him and an expert to explain each step.

There are several different kinds of weaves, but the weave alone does not determine either the final appearance or the wearability of a fabric. The construction—the number of warp ends in both directions—must be compatible with the weave, and the way a fabric looks and wears will depend on both the weave and the construction. Many fabrics are a combination of more than one weave. What is sometimes called a Jacquard weave is not a weave but a process used in making woven patterns. This process, used for making damasks, brocades, and brocatelles, combines different weaves, and is dull on one side and shiny on the other.

You can judge something of the construction of a fabric by feeling it to determine whether it is solid or sleazy, and seeing how close the threads are. This may not be important for curtains, but it certainly is for upholstery or slip covers. Use your hands, your eyes, and your common sense in buying this type of fabric. If it is for upholstery and doesn't seem quite dense enough, be sure that it has a rubber backing, which will make it wear better and longer. If you are using a fabric that is reversible, be absolutely certain that you have the same side out, when seaming lengths for curtains. Experts have been known to mix the right and wrong sides, which isn't apparent until they are hung. It is a good idea to double-check.

There are a number of different weaves, often divided into tight weaves and loose weaves. The only genuine tight weave is the *plain* weave, in which single threads go alternately over and under, just as you may try to make them do when you darn a sock. This weave is strong and durable, and with the right fibers and construction, is suitable for sturdy use. Taffeta is an example of a lighter plain weave, and upholstering linen of a heavy one. Two variations of a plain weave are a *rep* weave and a *basket* weave. When either the warp or weft is heavy and the other thread light, making a ribbed effect, it is called a rep weave. If more than one thread is used for both warp and weft (the same number), it is called a basket weave.

The most common loose weaves are twill, satin, and leno. The *twill* weave is made by a thread going under one and over two, producing a diagonal effect. Denim, serge, and flannel are examples of this weave, which may be fairly loose, or dense, depending on the construction. In the *satin* weave, as much as possible of the warp is left on the surface, making it smooth and lustrous. Satin is generally supposed to be made of silk, but it is a weave, not a fiber, and can be made from other fibers. Because it is so smooth, it has a tendency to catch on anything sharp and is not practical to have where there are animals. The *leno* weave is used for lightweight, open fabrics such as marquisette and net. Two warp threads are twisted around one weft in a kind of a rope effect, making a sheer fabric. It is sometimes called gauze, but is not. A gauze is a plain weave.

In *pile* fabrics, the process is different. There are two sets of warps. One makes a solid back, while the other goes over a wire and makes an upright loop. The loops may be cut or uncut. If cut, the result is a velvet or plush; if uncut, a frisé or terry. Pile fabrics are very durable. The smoother ones may spot easily but they can be processed for spot resistance. The heavy ones are exceptionally sturdy and long-wearing, and likely to be rather warm.

FIBERS

A fiber is a slender, fine-diameter single strand, from which yarn is spun. There are two basic groups of fibers—natural and man-made, which includes the synthetics. Natural fibers come from animals and vegetables. Cotton and flax, and to a much lesser extent, jute and hemp, are the most common vegetable fibers. Mohair, silk, and wool are the basic animal fibers. Man-made fibers include those made from: (1) chemically treated cellulose, (2) chemicals taken from other substances, (3) a protein base, (4) a mineral base, or (5) a rubber base. Fabrics used for decorating today are made of rayon and acetate from the first group; nylon, Dacron, and orlon from the second; and glass, from the fourth.

Natural fibers

Cotton.   Cotton comes from the bolls of the cotton plant, the fibers varying in length from less than an inch to more than two inches. The United States produces more cotton than any other country, but the finest cotton comes mainly from Egypt. Sea Island, Georgia, produces the longest and finest cotton fibers in this country.

In spite of all the synthetics, cotton is still used more than any other fiber. It is strong and durable. Many fabrics are made from it in a variety of styles and qualities. Technological developments in recent years have made it stronger and easier to take care of, and special processes have made it virtually colorfast. It is made into the finest and most luxurious kinds of fabrics and into the roughest and most functional. Since it is so well styled and so durable, it is used much more in the decorating of homes today than it was a few years ago. It also contributes its good qualities to blends with other fibers. In the past, cotton was often considered a "common" fabric. This no longer true.

Flax.   Flax, from which linen has been made for many centuries, is taken from the bark of the flax plant. The fibers are longer than those of cotton—sometimes as long as two feet. Linen has always been popular for tablecloths and napkins and for clothes, but today it is being used more and more for upholstery and curtains. Linens for decorating are available in interesting weaves, in both an array of solid colors and in many handsome printed designs. Linen is more expensive than cotton, but has most of its good qualities, plus a few of its own. It is more absorbent, stronger, and resistant to attack by mildew and bacteria. It is sturdy; for use as upholstery it can be treated to be more wrinkle-resistant.

Jute and Hemp. Fabrics made from jute resemble linen, but are much coarser and less resilient, and their use is limited. Jute was once used mainly for furniture webbing, carpet backing, and brown burlap bags. Burlap, today, has been softened and comes in a beautiful color line. It is used for curtains, wall coverings, and table mats. Hemp is harsh and coarse and can be made into only the coarsest kind of fabrics, few of which are used in home decorating.

Silk. Silk has always been considered—and still is, in spite of spirited competition by some synthetics—the finest fiber. Silk-making is a very old craft, probably developed in China at least two centuries before Christianity. The source of the fiber—the silkworm's spun cocoon—and the way it was made were both kept secret, and silk was not made in Europe until after the sixth century. The fiber is fine, lustrous, and very long —sometimes several hundred yards—and it is the strongest of the natural fibers.

Wool. Wool was known and used before any of the other fibers. Wool fibers come from the fleece of sheep and other animals—goats, llamas, and alpacas. For example, mohair, classed as a separate fiber by most manufacturers, comes from the Angora goat. It is often blended with wool and adds resilience, body, and wrinkle-resistance to a fabric. The length of a wool fiber depends on the animal and the length of time between shearings. Wool is a warm material and not particularly suitable for hot climates, but may be used with cotton or rayon to add strength or appearance. It is used less for decorating fabrics than most important fibers. It can be treated before it is woven into a fabric to make it shrinkproof and mothproof.

Synthetic Fibers. The synthetic fibers are made by a process similar to the one the silkworm uses to produce his filament. From its glands, a silkworm extrudes a liquid substance which solidi-

fies into a continuous filament, when it comes out into the air. Synthetics are made by three variations of a similar method. In each case, a solution is forced through tiny holes into warm or cool air, or a different solution, which solidifies it.

Because there are dozens of different synthetics known by hundreds of scientific and trade names, the most common trade names will be used here, and only those fabrics most important to decorating discussed.

Fibers Made from Chemically Treated Cellulose. *Rayon* is not a product of one person, or a single group, but of many. It was first made in the nineteenth century and the first industrial plant for the process started in 1910. A chemically treated cellulose, it was produced first as a substitute for silk. Today, it stands on its own.

There are two kinds of rayon—viscose and cuprammonium. The fibers of both are strong, absorbent, and receptive to dyes. The fabrics are mothproof and not affected by ordinary household bleaches and chemicals. A natural tendency to shrinking can be controlled in production. Rayon is the least expensive of the man-made fibers and blends well with other fibers. Viscose rayon comes in many forms, from a bulky, linenlike fabric, to a fine lustrous silky one. Bemberg—the name most associated with cuprammonium rayon—is slightly stiffer than the viscose and not made in as many forms. Bemberg is used mainly for clothing.

Acetate also comes from a cellulose base, but by means of a different process. It dries quickly, is resilient and wrinkle-resistant, and resists mildew and mold. When used as a drapery, it will not shrink or stretch and hangs exceptionally well. It is also less expensive than most other fibers and can be made in both sheer and heavy fabrics.

Fibers Made from Chemicals Taken from Other Substances. The name *nylon* is familiar to everyone and, since the Du Pont patent has expired, is used by several firms. There are also other registered trade-mark names for nylons. It is stronger, yet weighs less than any other fiber. It has elasticity and resilience. The fibers are non-absorbent and dry very quickly. Nylon is mothproof and can be washed or dry-cleaned. It can be woven to appear wool-like, or more like silk, and is often blended with other fibers to make them stronger. Nylon is used for many decorating fabrics, both alone and with other fibers. It is a versatile and practical fiber.

The *acrylic* fabrics are still known mainly by their trade names, of which the best known are Acrilan (Chemstrand), Orlon (Du Pont), Creslan (American Cynamid), and Zefran (Dow) —not a pure acrylic, but classed and used as one. The fibers may be light or heavy. The fine ones are soft and luxurious; the heavy ones feel like wool, and have the same kind of bulk. They are resilient, springy, strong, and resist sunlight, smoke, fumes, chemicals, moth, and mildew. They have low-moisture absorbency.

The *polyester* fibers are made into Dacron (Du Pont), Fortrel (Fiber Industries, Inc.), Kodel (Eastman), and Vycron (Beaunit). These fibers have been used primarily in clothing, but decorating fabrics are more and more being developed. They are wrinkle-resistant, easy to care for, quick drying, have good resistance to sunlight, and are quite durable. They are made into fine quality marquisettes and lightweight curtains. The fibers are also blended with cotton and rayon.

Saran also comes into this category. Called Rovana by the Dow Chemical Company who introduced the fiber in 1939, it is also made by Firestone (Velon), National Plastics Products Company (National), and the Southern Lus-Trus Corporation (Lus-Trus). It is nonflammable and resistant to sunlight and weather. It is less strong than the other synthetics fibers, but it can be washed and the colors are fast. It also resists chemicals, stains, abrasion, corrosion, and moisture.

Fibers Made from a Mineral Base.   Fiber glass is made by several different companies. It is nonflammable, will not shrink or stretch, and is not affected by sunlight. Fiber glass should never be dry-cleaned but is easily washable. The fabric is non-absorbent and dries immediately—as soon as the water runs off. It requires no ironing. Fiber glass is strong and holds color well. A disadvantage is its weight—twice as much as rayon, for example. On a large curtain, this makes what othewise would be easy hand washing difficult. It also has very low abrasion resistance and cannot stand rubbing against anything without the threads breaking. It can *not* be used for upholstery. The fabrics have been styled in a variety of handsome designs and interesting textures. Fiber glass is completely stable, does not shink at all,

and cannot be used with any fabric that will shrink.

Warning.   Federal law requires that all fabrics be labled with the fibers they contain. With an allowance that is very slight, for "other fabrics," the label must tell what percentage of fiber has gone into the manufacture of any fabric. You will always be able to tell definitely what fibers you are getting. If such a label is not on a fabric, don't buy it.

KNIT FABRICS

While woven fabrics fill the large majority of home-furnishings needs, knit fabrics are also available for certain purposes. For a number of years, knitted stretch slip covers, in both rayon and nylon, have been made. Their advantage, of course, is their flexibility in adjusting to furniture dimensions that vary slightly, and they are not expertly fitted. Not many of the knit fabrics have printed designs, but some nylon upholstery is knit and printed in such a way that it seems to be woven. These fabrics are functional budget items

More recently, a type of heavy casement curtain has been made from rayon in different kinds of knit patterns. It is practical for use where a material that is not sheer, and yet is not solid, is needed. There are some knit polyester sheers, but few of these are available in this country.

FELTED FABRICS

The use of felt has increased rapidly with the development of the product. A wall covering is available in beautiful colors, laminated to a backing to make installation more simple. It is fireproof, mothproof, colorfast, and will not stretch or shrink. An all-wool felt product called Wool Summa Suede (American Felt Company) comes in several handsome colors, made especially for upholstery. It is durable and will wear well. Feutron (American Felt Company), a felted material of Dacron and viscose, is also made in a beautiful color line for curtains and table covers. It hangs beautifully, at a window or on a table.

VINYL FABRICS

In addition to woven, knit, and felted fabrics, there is now available a family of vinyl fabrics. They are made in two ways—as vinyl sheeting and "supported" vinyl. Vinyl sheeting is vinyl pressed into broad, smooth sheets, in plain colors and textures, embossed, or printed in patterns. When vinyl is laminated onto a plain fabric (often a knit one), under heat and pressure, the two become one fabric, called supported vinyl. These vinyls are used for upholstery and wall coverings and can be handled as other fabrics. They are sturdy, flame-resistant, and can be wiped clean with a damp cloth.

SPECIAL PROCESSES

There are a number of special processes and finishes designed to make certain kinds of fabrics more practical for certain purposes. Two of these should be mentioned. The Scotchgard process makes fabrics resistant to water, colas, highballs, coffee, salad oils, baby oils, and other similar substances. Spilled liquids will "bead up" on a surface that has been treated, and can be blotted off. Scotchgard also processes fabrics resistant to ordinary dirt, and if they are wiped off occasionally, so the dirt can't get through the finish and into the fabric, they will show little soil.

Milium is the trade-mark of Deering Milliken and Co., Inc. for a process of metal-insulating fabrics. Practically any fabric of either natural or man-made fibers can be treated to make it keep out heat or cold. Milium is used on curtain lining fabrics and will keep out the heat of the sun in summer and the cold in the winter.

WHEN BUYING FABRICS

Practical Considerations. When you are ready to select a fabric, take the time to think through your choice in terms of function and appearance. Is the fabric appropriate to the function of the room? Don't put light-colored fabrics that will soil easily in a family room. A satin bedspread in a room where your daughter may be entertaining her friends who like to relax on the bed would be foolish. If the room is a dual-purpose one, be careful not to restrict your fabrics to a single purpose—try to keep them as flexible as you can. Remember the matter of maintenance. For rooms that get hard dirty use, fabrics that must be dry-cleaned are less practical than those that you can throw into your washer.

Design Considerations. Once you have given the performance careful thought, your selection of color and pattern should come next. Your reaction to patterns, printed or woven, is a response to design and color. When you are looking for a print, remember what you know about design and color in general. Choose patterns that have the right scale for the room; that are suitable in feeling. Be sure the fabric itself is suitable. Consider all colors in all kinds of lights—in the room where the fabric is to be used, if possible. The variety of printed and woven fabrics is almost unlimited. You can find anything you want—from the most bizarre kind of an abstract modern pattern in wildly contrasting colors to the most luxurious handwoven silks in the subtlest kind of design and color.

There is no law against using more than one patterned fabric in a room—but if you decide to do it, see that the patterns look well together. An expert may combine three—or more—in one room. But he knows how to do it and maintain a unified whole. Too little design may be better than too much and is certainly safer. If your colors are soft, you can probably use more design. Remember when you are buying patterned material for curtains that it will not hang flat—but in folds—and look at it that way. And avoid too emphatic a pattern for upholstery or slip covers. Remember that you will see it flat, and get the full impact. Generally, a bold design should be chosen in colors that harmonize. For a fragile design, sometimes you may want to use brighter colors, with more contrast.

Performance Considerations. Other things to be considered are the quality of the fabric and the color itself. If the fabric is washable, is it preshrunk? Does it have a guarantee of colorfastness? If so, what kind? There are many promotional statements that sound good on quick reading, but that say almost nothing when you get them home and read them carefully. Read all labels carefully and ask questions. If the fabric has any special finish, check to see what it is. Will it last through laundering or dry-cleaning? How long?

BE SURE TO CHOOSE THE RIGHT FABRICS

Fabrics are more personal than furniture and you should have a lot of fun shopping for them and getting them in your home. But they represent quite an investment and they won't be a source of much pleasure, unless you select them so they do their job and please you by their appearance at the same time. Go shopping when you feel fresh, never when you are tired. As with everything else you are getting for your home, plan carefully, consider the matter from every angle, do a thorough job of shopping—and then enjoy the results.

CHAPTER NINE

FURNITURE

PLAN YOUR BUYING THOUGHTFULLY

Some homemakers find the business of selecting furniture pleasant and satisfying. Others consider it a real chore. Whether you fit into the first group or the second, owning furniture will be neither pleasant nor satisfying, unless your selections are carefully made. Before you set out to look for any furniture, check your budget, review your floor plan, and find out all you can about the kind of furniture you will be looking for. Never buy impetuously.

Requirements. Any piece of furniture you buy should be: (1) well designed, (2) made of quality materials, (3) soundly constructed, and (4) well finished. These features should be combined so that the desk, chair, table, or whatever you are getting, is suitable for your purpose and consistent with your room design. If you are adding to a room already in existence, be sure that the new piece or pieces will not disrupt or destroy the unity of the room. If you are designing an entire room, select pieces that will be harmonious, used together.

TWO KINDS OF FURNITURE

There are two basic kinds of furniture: case goods and upholstered pieces. Case goods is the name generally applied to tables, desks, wooden chairs or benches, bookcases, cabinets, and any kind of storage pieces made from a variety of materials. Wood is by far the most commonly used—in solid, plywood, or veneer. Metals and plastics are also used and all of these materials can be had in many different finishes. Upholstered pieces include chairs, sofas and other furniture covered with fabric, leather, or other decorative material.

CASE GOODS

Tables. It wouldn't be at all surprising if, in your home, you had a dozen tables serving almost as many functions. Tables are used to hold lamps, books and magazines, glasses, teacups, or ash trays, or almost any object that one doesn't put on the floor. They are used for dining, for writing, and for games. Each table must be chosen for its particular function.

A table should be the proper size and shape for its purpose. With the fantastic diversity of design—from a step table or a butterfly drop leaf, to a modern rectangular table with a glass top and metal legs—there can rarely be a good reason for using the wrong kind of table. The material should also be suitable—for the purpose, as well as for the appearance. Some tables carry very light loads and don't need to be strong. Others not only carry heavy loads but will be worked on and must be well made, sturdy, and the right height with structural supports placed so they will allow sufficient legroom.

The height of a table may vary from fifteen inches (or even less)—the height of an average sofa seat and a convenient height for a coffee table—to twenty-eight or thirty inches, a comfortable height for a dining table. When a table is used for dining, writing, or games, the height

Fig. 96 Dining-room tables: *top left* French, *top right* English pedestal, *bottom left* English drop-leaf, *bottom right* modern.

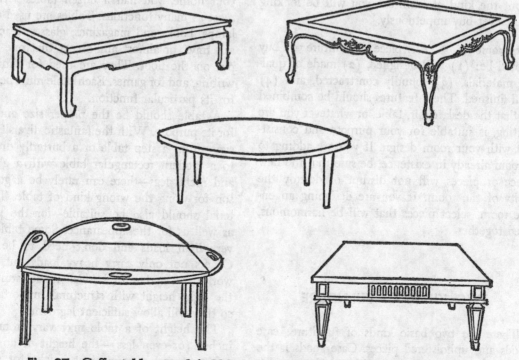

Fig. 97 Coffee tables: *top left* Chinese, *top right* French, *center* modern, *bottom left* English butler's tray, *bottom right* Italian.

should be determined in relation to the chairs that are to be used with it. The seats of most side chairs are eighteen inches from the floor—a good height for most tables, but be sure to check both legroom (at least five inches) and the height of the surface. A card table is generally quite low (twenty-seven inches) so that cards can be dealt and played easily; a desk is usually higher to bring the work surface closer and, sometimes, to allow room for a drawer. A dining-room table often allows more legroom than other tables. (See Fig. 98.) Co-ordinate table and chair heights.

If one or more of your tables must serve a dual purpose, be sure to select one that will qualify. Drop-leaf tables have been in use for several centuries, but are hard to beat as an attractive, functional piece of case goods. A well-designed drop-leaf table will always look nice and its flexibility—as a spacesaver that can be easily transformed into a comfortable dining table—is hard to beat. Console tables to which leaves may be added are also useful. But don't forget that this kind of table requires easily accessible storage space where the leaves can be kept. A console table is also much more difficult to change from its compact form to dining size than a drop leaf, and it is sometimes impossible for one person to do it alone.

Coffee tables can be functional in most any shape. Square, round, rectangular, oval, free form —choose the shape for your function, your space, and your design tastes. Where space is limited, it is usually best to have a coffee table that has no sharp corners, since the height of the table is such that it can inflict a painful bruise. Don't make the mistake of selecting a large coffee table if you don't have plenty of space: the function can be taken care of without the table being oversize.

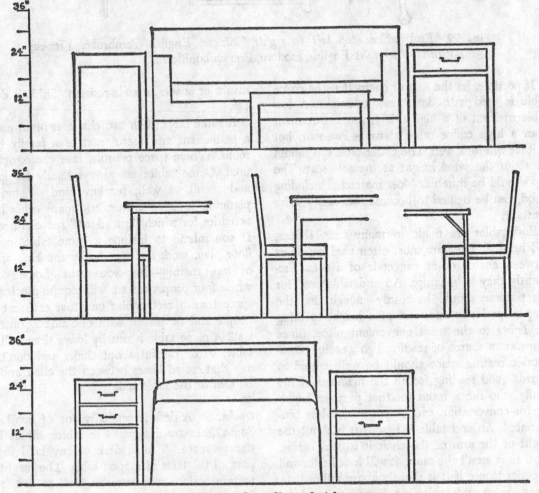

Fig. 98 Co-ordinate heights.

Fig. 99 End tables: *top left to right*: Chinese, English Pembroke, French; *bottom left to right*: English, modern, French bouillotte.

If possible, let the sofa or chairs that the coffee table is used with determine its height. A low table in front of a high sofa is more convenient than a high coffee table above a low seat, but neither will look well. The coffee-table top should be about the same height as the sofa seat. The top should be durable. Most materials, including wood, can be treated to become reasonably stain-resistant.

End tables are made in many sizes, shapes, and heights. They are most often used beside or between chairs, or at the ends of a sofa. Frequently they hold lamps. An end table used for this purpose should be sturdy enough that the lamp is perfectly safe, and of a height to bring the lights to the most convenient place. Since lamps are a source of reading light, enough comfortable seating space should be well lighted to provide good reading for all the members of the family who use a room for that purpose. Lighting for conversation can be softer and less concentrated. An end table is best if it is about the height of the arm of the chair it is used beside, but if they aren't the same, it will look better and be easier to use if it is slightly above rather than below. Since end tables are frequently used for

drinks or snacks, a stain-resistant finish is desirable.

A game table, with two chairs, is often used as a permanent and useful part of a family living room. Where space permits, four chairs may be used. Game tables are always handy for games and useful, as well, for any kind of studying, planning, informal eating, and many other home activities for which "spread-out" space is needed. If you intend to include a game table in your floor plan, work out specifically the kind—shape of top, mainly—that you want. Square ones, where four people can sit, will require much more space than a rectangular one that can seat two people and be placed with one side against the wall. A game table is usually lower than a dining table, so be careful about chairs and don't use any that crowd knees between the chair and the bottom of the table top.

Desks.   A desk is generally one of two kinds. Some desks are designed like tables; others have storage space. A table desk of any kind should pass all the tests of a good table. The height for writing surface may vary an inch or two, so it is important to choose desk and chair so they

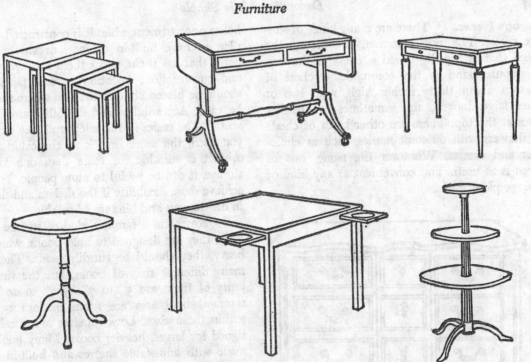

Fig. 100 Miscellaneous tables: *top left to right* modern nest, English sofa, French; *bottom left to right* English pedestal, modern bridge, French tier.

will be comfortable, used together. Styles of desks vary so much that it is difficult to generalize. But whether you have a Governor Winthrop or a one-drawer flat top, a desk has one main function —to provide a convenient place to write. Any desk should be sturdy, with a smooth, solid area for writing. The amount of storage space is determined by the style of the desk—and you have a wide choice. If there are doors or drawers, be sure that they move smoothly and fasten easily.

Fig. 101 Desks: *top left* modern, *top right* French slant top, *center* English secretary, *bottom left* English pedestal, *bottom right* French table desk.

Storage Pieces. There are many kinds of storage pieces. The most common, of course, is the piece that is broadly called a chest of drawers. A popular kind is the commode, a chest of drawers about thirty inches high, with two or three large drawers, and sometimes two smaller ones at the top. There are other kinds of chests of drawers with different names, such as chiffonier and dresser. Whatever the name, one of these is as useful and convenient as any kind of storage piece made.

Fig. 102 Commodes: *top* French; *bottom* English.

A cabinet is a storage piece with doors, which usually has shelves or vertical divisions inside. Cabinets are often made with doors below and two small drawers above. Many modern pieces combine units of drawers with cabinet units. Frequently this kind of furniture is built into a house or apartment when it is constructed. If you plan to have built-in cabinets or are buying a home that has them, check them for convenience and construction. Location is important. They should be placed close to the area where they will be used. Accessibility and flexibility are also essential. The easier it is to select and take out what you need, the more functional the cabinet. If a cabinet is suitable for more than one kind of storage, it can be useful to more people. You can achieve more flexibility if the shelves and dividers in the drawers and bins are adjustable.

Bookcases are a familiar kind of storage piece. Since they are designed to hold books, which are heavy, they should be sturdily made. There are many different sizes of books, but the vast majority of them are 5" to 7" by 7" to 10", and standard bookcases are often made for books within these sizes. Lower shelves are usually designed for larger, heavier books. Many bookcases made with adjustable shelves and built-in bookcases can also be made with strips that permit adjustment. Open shelves are attractive and practical for books that are frequently used. The dryness of winter heat and dirt may be hard on books kept in uncovered shelves, so judge for yourself which kind is most practical for you.

Judging the Construction of Wooden Case Goods. Good case goods must be well designed, carefully made of good materials and properly finished. How can you judge about all of these aspects? For the design, you should now be able to apply the basic principles with a fair degree of confidence. A variety of materials is used in furniture construction. Walnut and mahogany are two of the finer woods. They are both used in living-room, dining-room, and bedroom pieces, and in modern design as well as traditional. They are strong and durable, and can be finished in several different ways. These woods are rarely found in inferior pieces of furniture.

Maple and harder qualities of birch are used for their superior structural qualities, since they wear well and are hard enough to resist denting. They also provide a handsome wood finish. Ash, softer birch, and gumwood are structurally strong and are often used in combination with veneers of other woods, since they do not take as fine a finish.

The relative merits of solid wood, plywood, and veneers depend on the use. Solid wood must

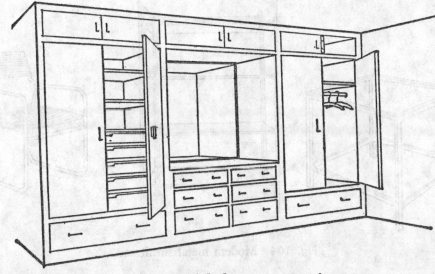

Fig. 103 A bedroom storage unit.

be used for furniture parts that are to be carved and for certain structural parts. Many fine pieces of furniture are made from solid woods. Plywood consists of thin layers of wood, glued and pressed together, with the grains at right angles to each other. Plywood is stronger than comparable solid wood, permits matching of grains, and can be used on curved forms. Veneer is made by gluing thin sheets of wood onto thicker wood. Depending on how it is done, veneer may make a piece of furniture cheap or expensive. Properly used, with a fine piece of veneer and the right kind of glues, veneer makes the maximum use of beautiful grain and is often found in the finest furniture. Cheap veneer, put together with inferior glues, will not stand up for long and will soon crack and peel.

Check the finish on the surface. Is it even, smooth, and free from marks of any kind? Does it appear to be hard enough to withstand use? Ask as many question as you can think of about how it was put on. The finest finishes are done by hand, but some good ones combine machine and hand rubbing.

What about hidden surfaces and joints? Several different kinds of joints are used in putting furniture together. The proper type of joint and the right kind of glue are both important, but are likely to be too difficult for the average person to evaluate. But you can turn the piece over and inspect the back. Are the surfaces here smooth? On the finest furniture a light coat of finish is usually used on backs and bottoms of case goods.

On less fine ones, all surfaces should be smooth. Are exposed ends finished to prevent chipping?

You don't need to know anything about design to check and see whether joints are perfectly matched, smooth, and tight. Watch out for careless construction and joints that have shrunk and been patched with wood filler or glue. Beware of gaps between joints. Screws are used in case goods, but there should be no nails. A table or wooden chair can be given the "wobble" test to see if it is well made. Rock one back and forth on the floor. A well-constructed one will stand firmly, without any wobble.

Check any areas where there will be special stress. Curved legs made of wood should be one piece. Check all drawers. They should have guide strips and should move smoothly. If they fit too tightly, they may stick in damp weather. The bottom of the drawer should be at least ¼" thick. Doors should open and close easily. Hardware on both drawers and doors should be of suitable design and scale for the piece of furniture they are on, and convenient to use. Some modern furniture has no hardware, but concealed finger-tip indentations are placed so the drawers are easy to open. The hardware, usually metal, on a traditional piece is very important to its appearance.

Metal Furniture.   Metal furniture has become increasingly popular in recent years and a wide variety of well-designed metal furniture is being made. From very simple modern, the designs go all the way to elegant and delicate designs based

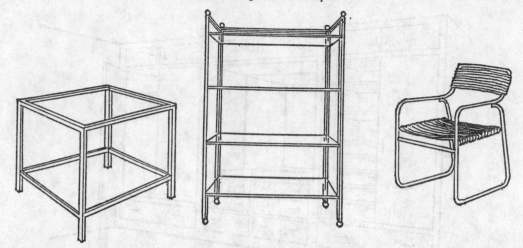

Fig. 104 Modern metal furniture.

Fig. 105 Traditional metal furniture.

on eighteenth-century furnishings. Aluminum and iron are the two metals most frequently used, and they are combined in an alloy in some pieces. Aluminum is rustproof and light, both desirable qualities. Iron can be treated to resist rust, but it is not light. Chrome, particularly in metal tubing, has been used widely in budget furniture. Stainless steel is growing in popularity for use as a furniture material, and is available in attractive designs. Since the metal is strong and can be thin, metal furniture can appear light in scale. It is easy to take care of and practical for areas where it will get hard use. Metal furniture has been used out-of-doors for many years, but today it is also being designed for use inside the home.

Plastic Furniture.   Plastics are being used for furniture, although not as commonly as metal. Modern chairs are made with molded plastic seats and backs. Plastics, which can be closely matched to the wood tone of a piece of furniture, are frequently used for tops on wooden case goods. They are durable, resistant to many things that will damage wood, and don't wear out. They are suitable when function is the primary concern, but they will never take the place of a surface of fine wood that has been finished by hand rubbing.

UPHOLSTERED FURNITURE

Construction.   Two upholstered chairs may appear to be identical. So much that is important to quality in an upholstered piece of furniture cannot be seen that it is almost impossible to judge by looks. You are able to see something of the construction of the frame by turning the chair upside down. In fine frames, no nails are used, corners are tight, and they are strengthened with corner blocks that are screwed and then glued for added strength. You can also see whether the hidden parts are smooth. This is usually a clue to quality.

In addition to the frame, you will want to find out all you can about the support for the seat, the springs, the filling, and the fabric that covers the chair. Seat bases should be reinforced and securely fastened to the frame. This will not be visible, nor can you see the springs that are used on top of it. You can tell something about both by the way the chair feels when you sit on it—but not enough. Your salesman is the only person who can explain about these hidden factors. Ask him all the questions you can think of.

Filling. Be sure that your salesman tells you exactly what kind of filling or stuffing has been used in any piece of upholstered furniture you are considering. Knowing what the material is

and how it is used can help you in judging its usefulness for your purpose. In the past, the finest filling (also the softest) was down, and next to that a combination of down and feathers. Quality, in this combination, varies with the amount of each kind of feathers used. Seventy-five per cent down to twenty-five per cent feathers is considered excellent, and a 50–50 ratio, good.

Today, although down and feathers are still used, foam rubber (made from latex), and urythene or polyester foam, both synthetics, are used for filling in a large quantity of upholstered furniture. In some pieces, two materials are used together. The advantage of these new materials is that they are comfortable to sit on, while at the same time have enough resilience to "come back," or to fill the cushion again after being crushed. Cushions filled with these materials have enough body and are sufficiently comfortable so they are often used without springs. They are placed on a piece of solid wood, or on some type

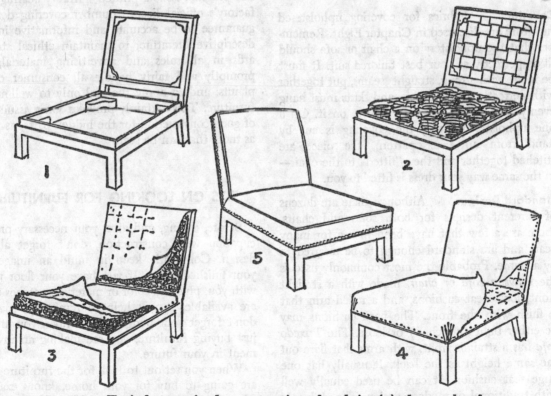

Fig. 106 Typical stages in the construction of a chair: (1) the wooden frame is completed; (2) webbing is attached to the back and seat, springs are added and tied; (3) hair filling is added to seat and back and covered with burlap; (4) a muslin cover is fastened over the burlap; (5) covering material is put on and fastened.

of a slat bottom, particularly in some modern chairs.

Most states have labeling laws requiring that all upholstered furniture designed for sleeping, resting, or reclining, be tagged with the contents of the filling. Such a law has been in effect in the state of New York since 1933. If a piece of furniture you are considering is not labeled and your salesman seems unwilling to tell you what it is, don't buy it. Rubberized hair, a combination of cotton-felt batting and hair, or feathers and kapok are used in some fairly low-priced budget chairs. Kapok is a vegetable fiber that is functional and comfortable for a limited length of time, but after a certain amount of wear, it turns to powder. None of these fillings will be as comfortable, or last as long as those listed above, but under certain conditions, they might serve your purpose. Your budget and the way you plan to use the piece, your salesman's expert knowledge, and your own sensible evaluation will all help to make your decision a right one.

Coverings.   Fabrics for covering upholstered furniture are discussed in Chapter Eight. Remember that the upholstery on a chair or sofa should fit as perfectly as your best tailored suit. It must be made with strong, straight seams, put together with perfectly fitted corners, and skirts must hang evenly, just to the floor—and never on it. On a fine upholstered piece, the covering is cut by hand from an exact pattern, the pieces are stitched together and then "fitted" to the chair—in the same way your dress is fitted to you.

Standard Designs.   Although there are dozens of different designs for both sofas and chairs, there are a few that have been in use for many years and are standard enough to be referred to by a name. Probably the most commonly used is the *Lawson sofa or chair*, made with a straight front, loose seat cushions, and a rolled arm that is flush with the front. The back cushions may be either tight (attached) or loose. The *Tuxedo sofa* has a straight front, with arms that flare out the same height as the back. It usually has one large seat cushion. It can be used equally well with traditional or modern design. The *club sofa* is often a heavier piece than either of the others and has a loose cushion on the seat, but may or may not have one on the back. The arms are a little lower than the Lawson arms and do not

come to the front, so the two side cushions extend in front of them.

A *club chair* is similar to the Charles of London design, with a loose, often T-shaped, cushion. A *barrel chair* is not as high as the average *wing chair*, it has a rounded back that is sometimes tufted or channeled. There are many different versions of the *wing chair*, but each one has a wing projecting on either side. Height of back or arm, and shape of back, arm, or wing, may vary. The seat may be tight, or made with a loose cushion.

Seal of Integrity.   The National Association of Furniture Manufacturers has set standards of quality and issued a "Seal of Integrity" to manufacturers in their group who qualify. The seal guarantees the item on which it is used to be "free from any defects in workmanship, material, and construction for a reasonable time, but not less than twelve months after delivery to the customer." The manufacturers who subscribe to this program issue a printed warranty bearing the factory's official license number covering defect; guarantee to be accurate and informative in all descriptive literature; to maintain ethical standards in all sales and advertising material; to promptly and fairly handle all consumer complaints; and to apply the seal only to well-made furniture. This certainly provides some assurance of good construction for the hidden parts, as well as those that can be seen.

TIPS ON LOOKING FOR FURNITURE

Before, during, and after your necessary preoccupation with construction, don't forget about design. Constantly keep in mind an image of your finished room. If you have your floor plan with you, plus any color or material swatches that are available, it will help to remind you. And don't forget your budget. Remember, you aren't just buying furniture, you are making an investment in your future.

When you set out to look for the furniture you are going to buy for your home, know exactly what you are looking for. Are you really trying to find something that will fill a need, or are you hoping to find a piece that you can fall in love with? More power to you if you find both in one piece. But too many people go to look for furni-

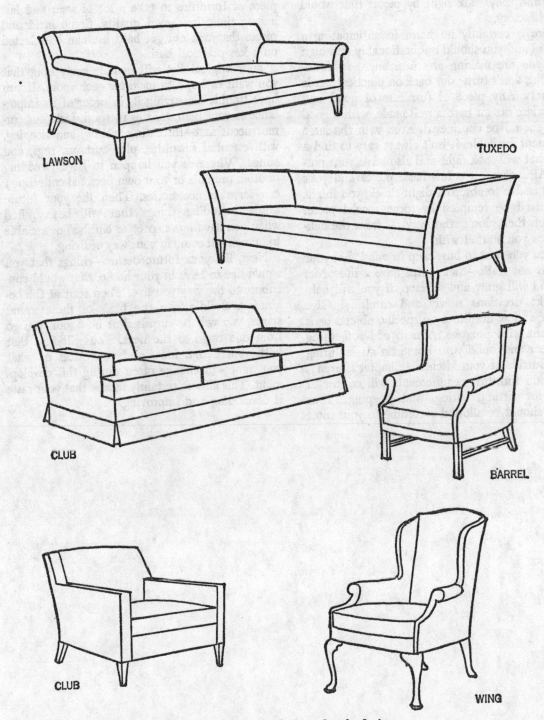

LAWSON

TUXEDO

CLUB

BARREL

CLUB

WING

Fig. 107 Popular chair and sofa designs.

ture hoping to be tempted or enchanted by some piece, and they walk right by pieces that would be satisfactory.

There is certainly no harm in anticipating a rare find and you should unquestionably aim high when you are making any investment in furniture. But, don't turn your back on practical needs and facts. Any piece of furniture of good and appropriate design that is well made, with a good finish, should be considered. Even with the large assortment available, it isn't always easy to find a piece that will look right and also serve your purpose. After you get a few basic pieces and your budget is able to absorb a slight shock, you might let yourself be tempted by some special piece. But even then, don't stray very far from the definite idea you started with.

When you start to buy, keep in mind that your home is not static—that it will have a life of its own and will grow and develop, if you will help it. Make decisions slowly and carefully. Give yourself as few deadlines on specific objects as is consistent with progress. Aim to add something each year and build your home on an enduring basis. Outside of your kitchen (Chapter Eleven), your main furniture requirements will consist of pieces for sitting, eating, and sleeping. Your budget should be allotted according to your most

urgent needs. And remember that if you want a piece of furniture to take a lot of wear and last a long time, buy good quality. Some incidental pieces that will not get hard use can be selected on a less practical basis.

Your original list will include everything that you want or hope to have for each room. If you have trouble classifying it, in order of its importance to your plan, try this method. List your current needs first—for eating, sitting, and sleeping, with essential furniture, plus curtains, rugs, and lamps. Whatever you happen to have (wedding or other presents or your own personal collection) can serve as accessories. Then list your future needs, including things that will be required when you have more space or children or are able to branch out some in your way of living.

Next, list your future desires—things that you would like to have in your home, that would contribute to the way you live. Then start at the beginning. Building on the basis of these sound stages, you will be surprised at how soon you go from one stage to the next. You will find that both your design ideas and your ideas of what you want will change often during this development. This almost certainly means that your taste is developing and improving.

CHAPTER TEN

ACCESSORIES—THEIR IMPORTANCE, SELECTION, AND USE

WHAT ARE ACCESSORIES—AND WHY

HAVE THEM?

What, in your home, do you consider an accessory? Accessory is a broad term that applies to many objects, but it doesn't embrace everything in a room that you have no other name for. An accessory is an object that helps in a secondary or subordinate way, and *adds* to the effectiveness of something else. Effectiveness may mean appearance or usefulness. As accessories are used today, even when they are functional, they are usually chosen with appearance in mind. The definition will serve notice that they should never be casually purchased or thoughtlessly placed.

What kinds of objects are classified as accessories? Pictures, and some mirrors, are among the larger ones. Books, clocks, vases, ash trays, candlesticks, screens, every kind of fireplace and desk equipment—all of them basically functional—also qualify. Ornamental objects, made mainly for the sake of their decorative effect, are accessories, and flowers and plants may be. A complete list would cover pages.

Why have accessories at all if they are secondary? Are they ever necessary? The second question is one that you must decide for yourself in your own home, but there are many reasons for having accessories. One of the most important reasons for adding these subordinate items to a room is to complete or highlight some special aspect of the design. You may want to call attention to a color in one area—just the job for the right accessory. You may have a small space conspicuously empty. An accessory can provide precisely the right interest.

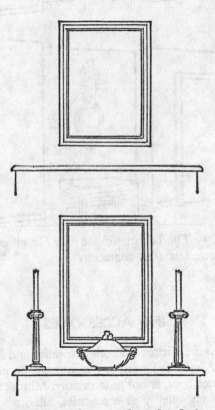

Fig. 108 Accessories complete the design.

Accessories can also add character to any room and are one of the best means of expressing your personality. They give you an opportunity to show cherished objects that you have collected. Displayed tastefully, these objects can add much to a room. A discussion of a few important categories, and of arrangement, should help you to place your accessories so they will have a reason for being where they are. (Lamps, which have an important function, are rarely secondary, are not classed as accessories, and will be covered under Lighting in the next chapter.)

the wall. Mirrors, large or small, can brighten a dark area, serve as a background for other accessories, and help to dramatize your design.

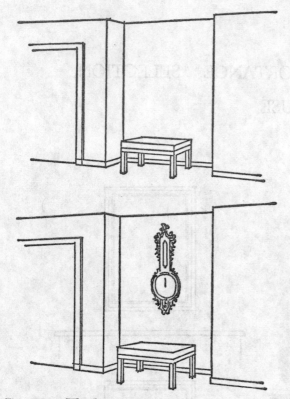

Fig. 109 The barometer not only fills an empty space, but adds character.

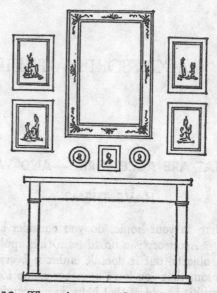

Fig. 110 The mirror-console combination makes an attractive center of interest.

USING ACCESSORIES

Mirrors. Mirrors are both decorative and functional. A mirrored wall, or a mirror on the inside of a closet door, is not an accessory. Mirrors used decoratively qualify as accessories, although this doesn't mean that they aren't useful. As accessories, mirrors should be placed where they will reflect something attractive and where they can be looked into (not too high). The design of the frame should be consistent with the design of the room, and the shape of the mirror must be suitable for the shape of the background against which it is used. A mirror with an especially beautiful frame should be placed in such a position that the frame can be seen and appreciated. If you don't want a frame on your mirror, there are several ways of having the glass attached directly to

Fig. 111 *Above* the wrong mirror. *Below* the right one.

Pictures.   Pictures used in homes today may be paintings—in oil, water color, tempera, or casein; drawings—in pencil, ink, charcoal, or pastels; or reproductions of any of these. (Don't be afraid of a good reproduction.) You can also get etchings, engravings, lithographs, prints of all kinds, wood or linoleum cuts, as well as many pictures produced by a combination of methods, or one of the less common techniques. The variety of subject matter is even greater than the kind of picture available, so there is really no excuse for you to have any pictures in your home that you don't like and enjoy—unless you do it to please some other member of the family. Pictures are personal, reactions to them are emotional, and they should not be hung if you do not truly like having them there to look at.

Framing.   Once you have selected a picture that you like, the framing and hanging must be carefully planned so the total effect will be one of good design. Scale, proportion, color, texture, decoration on the molding—all must be considered when you choose your frame. The various kinds of pictures call for different types of frames, but one statement is true of all. Don't let the frame compete with the picture. The frame should complement and enhance the picture and provide a transition between the picture, itself, and the design of the room.

Fig. 112 *Left* much too heavy and ornate a frame for the picture. *Right* the right frame.

Any good picture will suggest its own frame. Delicate water colors and pastels seem to need fairly light frames of soft wood tones or gold, while richly colored oils call for heavier frames, often carved and usually finished in wood tones—sometimes brushed with white or gold. Some pictures—water colors, prints, lithographs, etchings,

portrait photographs—are usually framed with mats. If they have a wide expanse of blank paper around the edge, mats aren't always needed. Almost any water color is improved by a mat and some that are unfinished at the edge require one. Most of these pictures are on paper and should be covered with glass for protection.

Oils are sufficiently protected by varnish, and glass need not be used. The beautiful and elegantly carved frames like those used for the paintings of the old masters are suitable for oil paintings of any kind. Paintings with abstract subjects are often framed with a severe, more modern, kind of molding, although antique frames are used for many modern paintings. This practice can be useful when tying in a very modern painting with traditional architecture in a room.

Mats.   When you take a picture to be framed, you will be able to try it with different kinds of mats. The mats may be of different-colored mat board, other more unusual kinds of paper (such as a marbleized one), or of fabrics, mirror, or glass. If you are using an average mat, don't let it be

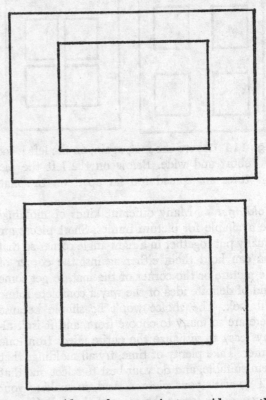

Fig. 113 *Above* the mat is too wide on the sides, too narrow top and bottom for picture. The mat below is suitable.

skimpy. For a picture that is 9½"×13", the mat should be 3" wide at the top and sides, and 3½" to 4" at the bottom. For a water color that is 14" by 19", the mat should be close to 4" wide at the top and sides, and 5" at the bottom. Larger ones can be 4½" or 5" top and sides, with at least an inch more at the bottom. (Sizes are all approximate.) A few pictures look well with narrow mats, but they are usually a special combination of mat with a wide frame.

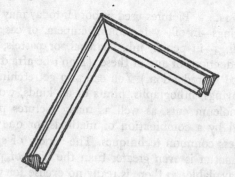

Fig. 115 A corner. Used to demonstrate the effect of a frame on a picture.

Fig. 114 *Above* the mat, again, on the left is too short and wide. *Below* on the left the pictures are spread too far apart on the mat.

Moldings. Many different kinds of moldings are available for picture frames. Short pieces are usually put together in a right-angle corner so that you can hold them either against the corner of the picture or the corner of the mat, to get some kind of definite idea of the way a complete frame will look. The choice won't be simple because there are so many to choose from, and it isn't always easy to visualize the entire effect from one corner. Take plenty of time, try all moldings that seem suitable, and do your best to select one that will go with your picture. And, in making your choice, don't forget the color of the wall (have a sample if possible), or the shape of the space where the picture is to hang.

Hanging. When you have a picture that you know you like, properly framed, you are ready to hang it. If you have had it framed for a particular spot, you will have a good idea of how it should be hung. But check to be sure that this one or any other is the right scale and the right proportion for the space. How does it fit into the composition of the wall as a whole? Are the colors right? If the answer is yes to all, hang it.

The height at which any picture should be hung will depend on the height of the room and the arrangement of furniture—but do remember that pictures are to be seen. Hang them where they will be as easy as possible for people to look at. When either a large picture or a mirror is hung over a piece of furniture, don't leave too much space between them. They usually appear best as a single unit. When pictures are grouped together, they should also appear as a unit. Don't leave too much space between them. The spaces can destroy the unity and make the arrangement appear spotty. It is a good idea to lay the pictures out on the floor—or on a table if you have one large enough—and take plenty of time juggling them around to make the best composition possible. Or you can cut pieces of wrapping paper the sizes of the pictures and, with bits of masking tape, try them on the wall in different arrangements. Usually, where you are grouping odd-sized pictures, it will help if you can keep a fairly straight line around the outside. When you hang a picture without furniture beneath it, be very careful that it doesn't appear to float in space. A painting should hang alone only when it is large and important enough to hold its own.

Books. Books aren't truly accessories, but are classified as accessories when used decoratively or

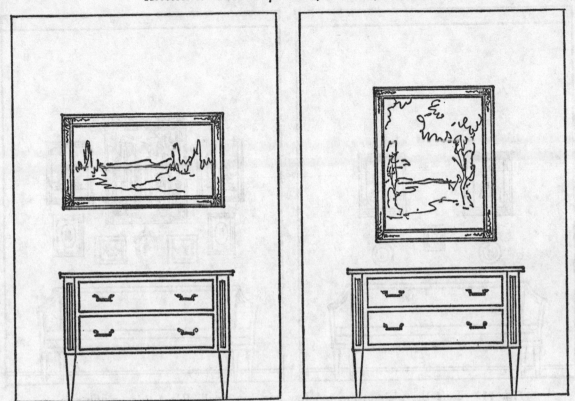

Fig. 116 *Left* the picture floats above the chest and there are too many horizontal lines. *Right* the picture is suitable.

in any large quantity in a room. If your bookcases are solid with books—no small decorative objects—the colors of the spines (backs of the books) and size should determine the arrangement. If there are small objects on the shelves, the books should complement them and help to provide an attractive setting. If you have more than one book with the same binding, or a set of books, use them as units.

Your shelves will not all be the same height. Put your heavier books on the lower shelves. If your bookcases are adjustable, as most of them are, you can arrange the shelves to suit the size of your books. Try to place the books so that no one stands out conspicuously. With so many brightly colored jackets, this may not be easy, but you can avoid sharp contrasts. Needless to say, the books you use most should be where they can be easily reached. Selecting books for their contents, and using them successfully for decoration, provides a double means of self-expression.

Ceramic Accessories. The materials from which accessories are made often give some clue to their use. The term ceramics applies to one of

the materials used in a wide variety of accessories, both functional and purely decorative. Unfortunately, the term ceramics has developed something of a craft connotation. Many interested amateurs work in ceramics for their own satisfaction. But this hobby work does not cover the meaning of the word. Ceramics includes all ware that is made from clay, shaped and hardened by heat. It is a broad term and according to an expert, ceramics, in relation to clay that has been shaped and fired, is as broad as the term metalwork in relation to all metals. The type of ingredients and the method of making and firing determine the kind of ceramics.

Pottery. According to some authorities, pottery and ceramics are synonymous. But top authorities do not agree with this opinion. Pottery is not a generic term, but is less broad. Pottery is similar to earthenware. They are both made of coarse clays, are fired at a lower temperature than other ceramics, and are heavy, soft, porous, and opaque. Usually thinly glazed, they are not often waterproof and are easily broken. A piece of either can be decorative, if suitably used, but it is not

Fig. 117 *Left* the pictures are too few and too small. *Right* this grouping is impressive and suits the space.

likely to be very fine and will probably look out of place in any but a simple setting.

Stoneware. Stoneware, on the other hand, while it may not be fine, has more quality. It is fired at a higher temperature, will hold its shape during firing, is nonporous, waterproof, and hard. It may be white or colored. Some of the early stoneware, which is still in use, had a lustrous brown glaze. It is sometimes made with fairly fine ornament and has a broader use than earthenware.

Porcelain and China. Porcelain is the finest kind of ceramic. It is made of special clay, fired at a high temperature, is vitrified (made glasslike), and is nonporous. It has a hard glaze that gives it

Fig. 118 A balanced arrangement of books and accessories.

a high finish, is beautifully translucent, and more resistant to chipping than other kinds of ceramics. The finest dishes are made of porcelain.

The first porcelain used in the Western world came from China, and originally the two words, *porcelain* and *china*, meant the same. This porcelain was made from a special clay, kaolin, and it was many years before Europeans could discover the formula. In the meantime, not only was all the imported porcelain called china, but also the results of all the efforts to copy it. The French attempt to make porcelain resulted in a soft-paste pottery that had great charm—and was called china. It had ground glass in it and, when melted and fused, looked fine. But it was more difficult to model, held its shape less well when fired, and was not as hard as porcelain. The first true porcelain made in Europe was produced in 1806 at Meissen.

What we call china today may be some kind of a glazed ceramic that has some, but not all, of the qualities of porcelain, or it may be porcelain. Many handsome designs are made in these various kinds of ceramic and if the ware is hard enough to be practical and the design right for your purpose, it may be as suitable as true porcelain. Whether you are buying dishes, a vase, a beautiful figure, or some abstract decorative object, know what kind of material you are getting.

Glass, Wood, and Leather Accessories.   Glass can provide certain effects that no other substance can. If you need an object that will catch and reflect light, and is transparent, glass may be the answer. But it is often fragile. Many beautiful accessories are made from wood, which has a warmth that makes it especially desirable in some schemes. It also has its own decorative quality, in the grain, and the choice of colors is wide. Whether you choose a softly curved somewhat bulky piece, a sharply angular abstract, or a finely carved medieval figure, depends on your taste and the place it is to go. Leather, which also has a warmth and softness that few of the other materials have, is used for desk equipment, wastebaskets, a variety of attractively designed boxes, and other objects.

Metal Accessories.   If you like your accessories unbreakable and strong, you will find that metals are practical. Several metals, in different finishes, are commonly used. Some give a feeling of warmth, others are cold. A shiny silver finish is

cooler and reflects more brilliantly than a soft, or satin finish. Pewter is slightly warmer in tone and is less highly polished than silver. Copper and brass have very definite color and, although the finish will affect the color to some extent, either should be chosen only if the colors it is to be used with are harmonious. Aluminum, used decoratively in its natural color, more often has a satin finish than a shiny one and, when suitably designed and used against the right background, can be very effective.

Plastic Accessories.   Certain varieties of plastic are also used for accessories. When made into designs appropriate to the material, they can be very handsome. Some of the decorative plastics have been used with honesty and character, depending on no kind of traditional design for their inspiration, and are beautiful. Others are simply attempts to imitate natural materials and are definitely inferior. There can be no valid reason for using pseudo materials for accessories, unless function is of basic importance.

Fireplace Accessories.   Fireplace equipment should be selected carefully as part of the mantel composition. Fortunately, since you take your fireplace furnishings with you when you move, and don't take your fireplace, many designs look well in a variety of fireplaces. Nevertheless, your andirons, screen, tools, and fender or grate look best if they are of the same kind of design as your chimney piece. Period furnishings or suitable modern designs can be found to go with the architecture of most mantels. It isn't really necessary that all the fireplace accessories match, but they should be compatible. Unless the scale and proportion of your equipment is agreeable, it will probably be a good idea to sell whatever is badly scaled and replace it. A fireplace is usually an important spot in a room and it is a mistake to assemble its furnishings in any but truly good design.

For rustic, and many modern or provincial, fireplaces, iron equipment is likely to be appropriate. Designs executed in iron range from rough to somewhat ornate. The material and style of the mantel will help you to decide. A heavy stone fireplace, for instance, is probably much better fitted with strong iron fixtures of good scale than with delicate ones. For the finer kind of traditional fireplace, either iron with brass trim or brass fix-

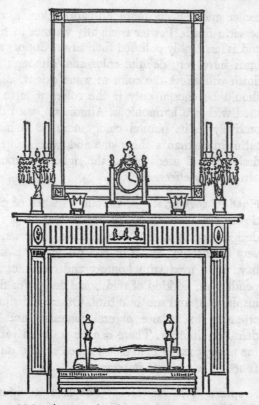

Fig. 119 Accessories for a traditional fireplace.

tures will probably be more suitable. As with everything else in decorating, it is a matter of combining pieces that have in common a general design feeling, scale, proportion, and using colors that harmonize.

Flowers and Greens.   The way you use flowers as accessories will depend on what you like, what is available, and the places where you use them. Avoid artificial greens unless you are really desperate. On the whole they are not very beautiful, and once the dust begins to settle on them, they appear tasteless, without any character. Expensive—and sometimes beautiful—artificial flowers can be found in shops. Use them as a last resort and don't let the same arrangement sit in one place for several weeks. If you have a variety of nice ones, you can arrange them with fresh greens, (only when fresh flowers are not available or are too expensive) and leave the arrangement for about the same length of time that fresh flowers would last. The fresh greens give them a fresher look and if you don't leave the artificial flowers long enough to get tired and dirty, they will seem much nicer the next time you pull them out to use. They can dress up your house for a special

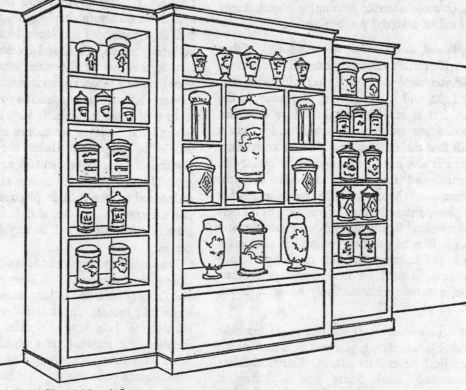

Fig. 120 A large collection displayed in open cupboards.

occasion, and used only that way, they can prove a good investment.

Fresh flowers from the garden make the nicest kind of special decoration in a room. If you are interested in highly styled flower arrangements, make a study of them and know what you are doing. If you like to arrange flowers casually, don't crowd too many into one vase, and be sure that the colors you are using look well together and against the colors of the room in which they are being used. Don't put a tall, top-heavy bouquet on a low table where someone is sure to knock it over. Low, full bowls are better in such places. Combine the colors, the shape, and the general kind of design to look well together—is the arrangement elegant, gay, simple or severe?—with the background where it is being used.

Collections. Do you have a collection that you are fond of and would like to show in some room? If the collection is an interesting one, and you can arrange it to look well, you certainly should give yourself the pleasure of displaying it. A small collection can be shown in a part of a shelf, as a unit, with books or other objects arranged to set it off. For larger collections, cabinets, cupboards and wall shelves can be used. If you have chosen small enamels or coins, they can be mounted on a backing and framed, then arranged together on a suitable wall space. Make your collection seem of major importance in the area where you show it. Be sure that it harmonizes—in both color and form—with its background, and if possible, feature it by lighting. If it is beautiful enough, it can serve as the center of interest in a room. It certainly is personal, and showing it provides an opportunity for you to express yourself.

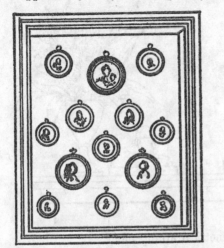

Fig. 121 A small collection well displayed.

SELECTING ACCESSORIES

In many homes today, there are fascinating accessories from a far country that were not purchased at some local gift or specialty shop, but in the country where they were made. With increased tourist travel, hundreds of foreign grants of many kinds, and government jobs and military service all over the world, it is no surprise to go into any average home and find objects from almost any country. With these original sources as competition, local shops have been forced to carry a far more interesting stock of better quality.

Anyone who has bought articles of this kind in the country where they are made and used will have a far better understanding of their use and appreciation of their value than if they had been purchased a few blocks away. This trend, plus the greatly increased exchange of ideas through all kinds of communication media, has altered the meaning of many accessories. They are rarely seen used in the variety of unsuitable ways they once were.

Since the choice is such a wide one and personal tastes so varied, it is impossible to formulate any specific rules for selection. But this is a time when, most emphatically, impetuous buying should be sternly avoided. If you see something that you really can't resist—that you *know* you will continue to enjoy ten years later but still, at the moment, you can't figure out where to use it—go ahead and get it. The chances are that you will find a good place. But don't let yourself go—ever. It is much better to have a place to be filled and choose something especially for that place, than to simply buy things that appeal to you. You can almost surely find things that will appeal to you and are *also* right for the place, if you will just spend a little more time looking.

It is not necessary for architecture, furniture, and accessories to come from the same design period. Scale, proportion, color, and general kind of design are more important. Accessories of some periods are similar to those of others, but as long as they are appropriate, even that isn't necessary. Aim for some variety and don't be carried away by an infatuation for some one type of object and find yourself oversupplied before you realize it. Think ahead every time you select any kind of accessory, and figure just how it will go with the room as a whole.

PLACING ACCESSORIES

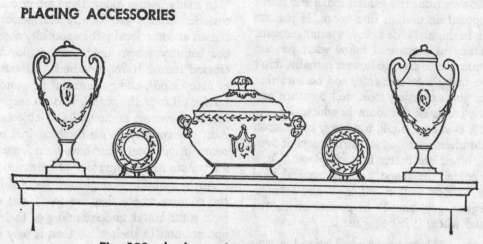

Fig. 122 An interesting symmetrical arrangement.

When it comes to placing accessories, remember that they are part of a larger whole—intended to add to the effectiveness of something else. Be sure they do add to it and do not compete with it. Be careful not to have too many isolated objects —and avoid clutter. The well-designed arrangement considers each space as part of the design. When you have several objects, feature some at the expense of others (center of interest and emphasis on a small scale) or none of them will show up to advantage. On a mantel or the top of a bookcase, whether your arrangement is symmetrical or assymetrical, have a definite center of interest and let the other accessories build it up. It may be a clock, a lovely bowl, a delicate figure,

or a piece of abstract sculpture; but arrange the other objects so the eye will instinctively go to the one you are featuring.

Accessories are often needed to provide color. Be sure to use the right color and the correct amount to do the job. If you have a space that needs a little color, plan very carefully. If you have the ill luck to find a furnished apartment that is colorless, your accessories can help to correct that. Suppose the walls are off-white, the floor is dark, and the furniture is dark wood upholstered in neutral-fabric tones. You can get a bright-colored abstract painting—a reproduction will do (or you can paint one yourself!). You like sharp blues and greens, so you will use variations of both, with

Fig. 123 A well-balanced asymmetrical arrangement.

accents of vermilion. Two or three small area rugs that pick up these colors in the design or the border, some bright cushions on the sofa, a green malachite box, and a few smaller accents in other pictures—and the room has been lifted out of its dreariness.

SUMMARY

You may have heard it said that accessories can make or break a room. Don't believe it. No sloppily designed room is really going to be salvaged completely by the best accessories in the world, nor can a beautiful room be ruined by bad accessories. But a beautiful room can be further enhanced by the proper accessories, and a badly designed room can be greatly helped.

The choice and placing of your accessories can help to make a room more, or less, formal. Simple, sometimes fairly heavy ones—abstract wood carving or pottery—are suitable in a casual room. In a more formal room, fine porcelains, silver, and etched glass will add to the elegance. The choice of objects, materials, kinds of design and colors is, literally, infinite. You can do much with them. But don't, ever, let yourself be casual on your basic design, on the theory that you can cover it all up and correct everything by the way you use accessories.

CHAPTER ELEVEN

LIGHTING AND EQUIPMENT

Importance of Electrical Equipment. In this technological age, you can choose whatever temperature you want, turn a knob, and the furnace or air conditioner will maintain it as long as you wish. You can leave home with your stove adjusted to come on at a certain time, at the exact heat you need. You can sit in your chair and change your television program by remote control or listen for hours to your favorite music, uninterrupted. And these conveniences aren't found only in the homes being built now. They can also be installed in older homes.

In this country, very few homes are without electricity, the main source of the power that keeps automation moving. You have only to read about what happens when the power in a community goes off for any length of time to be impressed by its importance. Much electrical equipment is concealed, but lighting fixtures, kitchens, and television sets are all very much in view, and should definitely come into the aesthetic, as well as the functional part of your planning.

LIGHTING

Sunlight is still the most important source of light. But since it is available only part of each day (and then in varying amounts), and cannot always be had where needed, artificial lighting has become indispensable in the average American home. Too often, lighting needs and the choice of fixtures are not given enough consideration in the over-all planning. Your home, no matter how beautiful it looks or how smoothly it functions in other ways, will not prove satisfactory unless it is properly lighted.

Electricity in the home, historically speaking, is comparatively recent. But the variety of design that has appeared in very recent years is almost beyond the comprehension of the average person. For instance, one type of ceiling light, called low brightness, can only be seen by someone almost directly beneath it. Looked at obliquely, this fixture shows no light, but it does illuminate the area it is designed to light. Another piece of special equipment allows complete brightness control. You can make room lights dim or brighter like the house lights in a theater.

Consult An Expert. There are many trained electricians to assist in keeping these modern fixtures in top operating condition. But don't confuse an electrician with a lighting engineer. Lighting engineers are specialists in planning and supervising the installation of the complete lighting of a home. An architect or your local lighting company may recommend one, or you can find him listed in the yellow pages of your classified telephone book. Modern lighting should be part of any house plan and should be installed when a house is being built. It can be added after the building is completed, or put into an older house, but not without making certain compromises. Whatever the scope or character of your lighting needs, it usually pays to consult an expert.

Potentialities of Lighting.   What should light do for a room? It should provide sufficient illumination for every need. This is the most commonly accepted function, but there are many others. It adds greatly to the safety of a home. It can open up space, making it possible to use all that is available. It can also help set the mood, or influence the general feeling of a room. The right kind of low, diffused lighting can make a room seem restful. Bright light can help to provide a stimulating atmosphere that contributes to energetic activity. Emphasis is achieved through spot lights or special effects; mystery through dimly lighted areas; decorative effects through strategic placement.

Color tones of walls, rugs, furniture, or curtains can be featured or softened. Colored bulbs can also help to produce other desired effects, such as changing the color of a lamp shade. For example, if a transparent shade appears to be too cold a white, a warm-colored bulb will alter the color. If it is a blue-green with too much blue, a yellow bulb will take the sharpness from the blue, making it greener and softer.

Functions of Lighting.   There are three main functions that lighting should perform: (1) task lighting, (2) general illumination, and (3) accent lighting. The task light should make easier the performance of activities that need practical, concentrated light. Work counters, kitchen sinks, reading areas, desks, and bathroom mirrors are among the places that need good, efficient task lighting. General or area lighting should create a comfortable "seeing" environment. It is softer, less direct than task lighting, adds to the appearance of a room, and should be complimentary to the people in the room. It should provide pleasant lighting for conversation and general activities. Accent lighting, which includes the various kinds of spot lighting, creates focal interest in a room. It may feature a painting, or some special object or effect, and is basically decorative.

Kinds of Lighting.   The basic kinds of lighting make use of three general types of light: direct, indirect, and a combination of the two. Most lamps provide the first, which shine directly on the objects or area close to them. Many lamps also provide indirect light, with reflectors and bulbs above the direct light. In any kind of direct lighting, bulbs should be shaded to avoid glare. Direct lighting provides the sharpest contrast between

light and dark (not necessarily desirable) and makes the most dramatic shadows.

Indirect lighting is secondary light and comes from the reflection, on the ceiling or any surface, of light from an original source. It is diffused, softer, and much less dramatic than direct light and more useful for general illumination. The third kind makes use of both. A portable lamp—for table or floor—with bulbs both inside and outside of a reflector gives a well-known combination of both types. The bulbs in the reflector shine on to the ceiling and are reflected down, while those outside and below shine directly on the area below the lamp.

Kinds of Bulbs

Incandescent Bulbs.   The two different sources of light are incandescent and fluorescent bulbs. Incandescent means glowing, due to heat, and light is produced from the heating of the filament in the light bulb. The variety of incandescent bulbs available has been increasing at a rapid rate for some years and continues to do so. The size varies from three watts to 10,000 watts; and bulbs are made that provide three levels of brightness. There are many different shapes, including a tubular bulb.

The most familiar incandescent bulb is the standard frosted one which gives a warm light that is much pleasanter than the light given by the more familiar fluorescent bulb. There are many other colors. Floodlight-shaped bulbs, which are used both outdoors (100 watts), or indoors (75 or 150 watts), are made in seven colors—red, pink, green, yellow, blue-white, blue, and amber. Used indoors, different colors can be blended, creating unusual and beautiful effects. The pink and blue-white are very complimentary to skin tones. Yellow and amber can be combined to create an effect of sunshine. The red, blue, and green are very strong, are rarely used indoors, and are recommended only for rather spectacular effects.

Another series of colored bulbs is tinted—pink, blue, and gold, or green. These are for indoor use, and will accentuate certain colors or effects. By changing the color of your bulbs you can create a different appearance in a room. When using these bulbs (called Coloramic by General Electric), if you are replacing a white one, it is a good idea to get a bulb with the next higher wattage.

There are several different socket sizes for incandescent bulbs, but 95 per cent of those in use are the medium size that the average bulb fits into. Because bulbs of different wattage can be used in the same socket, and because of the convenient size and shape of the bulbs, incandescent lighting allows for more flexibility than fluorescent. However, it is much more expensive to operate, and even the new longer-lasting bulb lasts a relatively short time when compared with a fluorescent bulb which lasts for several years in normal home use. The incandescent lumaline bulb, a tubular bulb with contacts at both ends, looks something like a fluorescent bulb; intended only for decorative use, it is much more expensive, and is not suitable to use with a bathroom mirror.

Fluorescent Bulbs. A fluorescent bulb is a long, slender tube of translucent glass coated on the inside with special powders that glow under certain conditions, brought about by turning on the current. It is made only in tubular form—either straight or circular. If you can use either kind you will get much more for your money than you would with an incandescent bulb, since a fluorescent bulb gives approximately five times as much light as the same wattage in incandescent. The installation is much more complicated, and consequently more costly. But the bulbs are less expensive, longer-lasting, and have the added advantage—and an important one—of being much cooler.

Originally, fluorescent bulbs were all a cold white and there are more of this kind still in use than all others. Also, when they were first made, there was a lag between turning on and lighting, and they made a humming sound. Both of these weaknesses have been eliminated and bulbs now come in many colors.

The commonly used bulb is called Cool White. A De Luxe Cool White bulb is now made that gives a light similar to daylight. Warm White and De Luxe Warm White both do a better job of color rendition, similar to that of the incandescent. These Warm White bulbs should be used beside bathroom mirrors because the Cool White gives skin an unpleasant tone. Daylight, White, and Soft White are variations of the first white bulbs. In addition to these, fluorescent bulbs can be had in blue, green, pink, gold, red, and deep blue.

Using Bulbs. Often, the solution to a lighting problem requires a combination of both incandescent and fluorescent bulbs. All experts are in total agreement on one fact. With the exception of small flame-shaped bulbs, which are used decoratively in various kinds of fixtures, no bulb should *ever* be exposed. Glare, however, is not always caused by unshaded lights.

Lights in any room should be balanced—just as your furnishings are. For good general illumination, sharp contrasts should be avoided. One of the greatest causes of glare is the contrast between the bright light of a high-wattage lamp falling on a book, while another part of the room, a few feet away, is in relative darkness. General Electric has a number of booklets that can be helpful in illuminating your home, covering such things as the proper way to place lamps (distances, height, etc.), what each bulb can do, and types of structural lighting (valance, cornice, etc.). Literature is available from the lamp division of General Electric.

Fixtures. Your choice of lighting and fixtures depends on your needs and preferences, but the possibilities are infinite. You may want spotlighting from the ceiling; a fixture placed behind a valance over a window; cove lighting set into a depression just below the ceiling; or luminous panels made by using fluorescent bulbs behind translucent glass. Or you may prefer to have a wall or ceiling fixture, installed flush with the wall, recessed in the plaster, hung from the ceiling, or fastened to the wall. You may like switches in the closet doors, so the light goes on when the door opens and off when it closes, or special lights in shelves where accessories are displayed. Figure out what kind of lighting you think you need, and then, before you select your fixtures, consult a lighting expert.

If your room is traditional, you have a choice of good reproductions of fixtures of many periods, or you can often find old ones and have them wired. If you choose a reproduction, be sure it is right for the size, scale, and proportion of the room, as well as being design of the appropriate period. If you are having old fixtures wired, get expert advice. It is possible to completely destroy the beauty of a fine old fixture by wiring it in an unsightly way. A wide variety of modern fixtures of every type is also available.

Lamps. Lamps are the old, friendly stand-by for lighting in many areas of our homes. They go back far beyond electricity, but still serve much the same purpose that they always have—except that the lamps made today provide better light

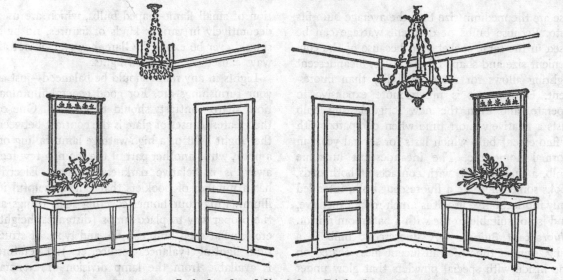

Fig. 124 *Left* the chandelier is lost. *Right* the scale is good.

than the earlier ones. Lamps can be beautiful (see that yours are) and contribute greatly to the attractiveness of any room. Beauty, in a lamp, is essential, but function is of major importance. A lamp functions well if the size, height, and location enable it to adequately light the particular area it is planned for.

The design of a room, to a large extent, should determine the kind of lamp design. Once you've

taken care of function, consider your choice on the same basis you did your accessories. For a period room, there are many suitable possibilities. A beautiful urn of the English Regency period, for example, can be wired and made into a lamp. Many accessories that are appropriate for the design of a room can also be converted into lamps. Often, if you look, you can find handsome lamps that are copies of fine old pieces of porcelain,

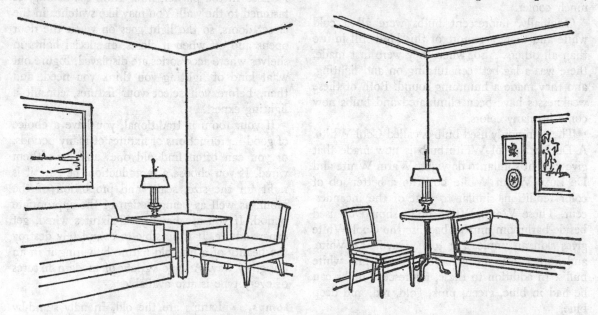

Fig. 125 *Left* the lamp is much too small for the table, too low for reading. *Right* it is well used.

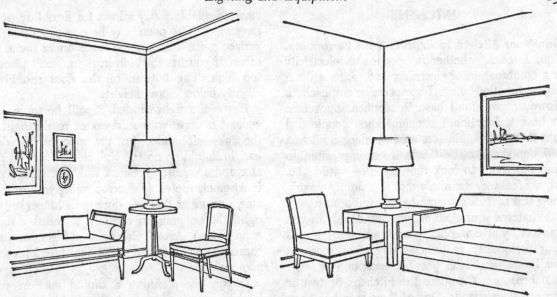

Fig. 126 *Left* the lamp is much too large for the other furnishings. *Right* it is used properly.

marble, silver, or some other material, that were used during a certain period.

Be careful not to give too much emphasis to lamps. In general, simplicity is a desirable quality in a lamp. Many modern lamps are the essence of simplicity. But remember that when you select a lamp base that is simple, the scale and proportion must be very good. Some very beautiful lamps—porcelain of the Louis XV period, or English silver, for example—may be very ornate. Judge the design on its own merits and by all means use such a lamp if it looks well in your room.

The proportion of the lamp base to the shade must be right. Whether the design is traditional or modern, lamp and shade should be seen as a unit. This is imperative. When you select a lamp in a department store, it is usually complete, and you are able to see exactly how the base and shade look together. If you are looking for a special kind of lamp and must buy the base separately, be sure to try whatever shade you get *with* the base. Unless you have tried another shade and know the exact dimensions you want, *never* select a shade without seeing it on the base.

Don't be afraid of large lamps. While there are places where small lamps are suitable—a dress-

ing table, some desks—in most locations it pays to think big. You needn't overdo it and use a carrousel horse for a base (as has been done); but a skimpy lamp looks terrible and often doesn't provide good light. Any place where you use a lamp that must provide illumination enough for reading or to light part of the area of a room, whether it is on a table or the floor, see that it is large enough and high enough to accomplish its purpose.

Lamp shades can be made of many different materials and they may be either opaque or translucent. They should not be fussy. Some restrained trimming may be used, but nothing that interferes with the performance of the shade. Leather, parchment (paper treated to look like parchment is more practical), heavy paper—with thin sheets of marbleized, gold, silver, or tortoiseshell paper mounted on it—are used for opaque shades; also some heavy fabrics, and metal, particularly tole or brass. Silk, rayon, nylon, and other lightweight fabrics are used over wire frames for partially transparent shades, although they are usually lined. The light from this type of shade is less concentrated and more diffused than light from an opaque shade. Plastics of various kinds are used for both opaque and translucent shades.

KITCHENS

Plan Your Kitchen to Express Your Personality.
Your kitchen, whether it operates on electricity
or a combination of electricity and gas, is a room
where function must be especially emphasized.
However, you don't have to sacrifice appearance
to have a functional kitchen. Some people feel
that the many appliances around which a kitchen
is designed make it difficult, if not impossible, to
plan the room to look the way they would like.
Others feel very definitely that it is simply a work-
shop and that its appearance isn't important.

Whatever your attitude, unquestionably, if you
want to, you *can* plan your kitchen to express
your personality as fully as any other room in
the house—with the possible exception of your
own bedroom. Compare the kitchens of two or
three of your friends. One of them may be warm,
hospitable, and colorful, with comfortable places
to sit for a cup of coffee. Another might be all
white, with appliances that are placed for the
minimum of waste space—a room where kitchen
work only is done. If you are building, about to
rent, or plan to make some changes in your
kitchen, approach the project in the same way
you approached the planning of other rooms.
Function must come first, here. But that doesn't
for one second rule out beauty.

Arrangement of Work Space.   If you are planning a new kitchen or changes in your present
one, the arrangement is most important. If your
problems are serious, it is wise to get some professional advice—from an architect, a kitchen
contractor, representatives of your local utility
company, or a qualified interior decorator. Otherwise, figure out what you need, work it out on
your floor plan, and then find out what is available that fills your needs.

Most kitchens have three major work areas—
around the stove, the sink, and the refrigerator.
It will save steps if they can be fairly close together, with the sink between the stove and refrigerator. Try to have counters on both sides of
the sink—two feet wide, if space permits—since
the sink is used both for preparing and cleaning
up. If you hope to have a dishwasher some day,
but can't install it at the beginning, allow space
for it next to the sink. You also need storage
space for cleaning materials.

The stove may provide some working surface,
but should adjoin counter space. The variety of

stoves available today allows for flexibility of arrangement. The oven may be one place and the
surface units, with storage space under them, another. If you have a built-in oven, don't place it
too high. The bottom of the door should be
slightly below elbow height.

If you are right-handed, it will be more convenient to have your refrigerator to the right of
the sink—left-handed, just the opposite. The door
handle should be on the sink side of the refrigerator and a counter between sink and refrigerator
is extremely useful. (When selecting your refrigerator, remember that the door with hinges on the
right, the opening on the left, is called a right-
hand door.) Avoid placing a refrigerator in a
corner or any place where the door interferes with
another door.

If you are planning a dining area in your
kitchen, have it as far from the work area as space
permits. It will be pleasanter and make for more
relaxed eating if it isn't close to the hot stove,
counters where soiled pans may be left, or the
sink where water may splash.

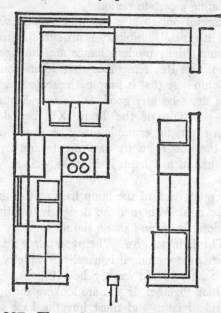

Fig. 127 Floor plan of a well-designed kitchen.

Hints About Cabinets.   There are cabinets to
suit every taste and every design requirement.
You can have natural or painted wood, with
hardware that is concealed, or made of wrought
iron. You can have enameled steel—white or colored. You can even have metal cabinets that look
like wood. All types come ready-made in a wide
variety of sizes and shapes, with many different

kinds of arrangements for storage. You can also order cabinets custom-made to your own specifications, or have a local carpenter do the job. You can certainly have whatever kind of kitchen you want; your only limitations are space and money.

Your cabinets will be more practical if the shelves are adjustable. Two shallow shelves (be sure to allow space for your hand to move things on the shelf easily) are better than one deep shelf where dishes are stacked. Doors should open and close smoothly, since you often need to move them when your hands are wet or sticky. Drawers should be made with no cracks, to avoid catching crumbs. They should also open easily, and have some kind of a stop to keep them from coming all the way out. The ease and speed with which a full drawer comes out can carry it right to the floor if there is nothing to stop it. Special sections for trays, storage space for appliances not kept on the counter, and a handy drying place for towels should be included in your plan.

Lighting.   Lighting is very important in a kitchen. You will certainly want some general illumination—a fluorescent fixture in the ceiling is practical. You will also need area lighting for your work spaces. Your lights should enable you to see all the way inside your cupboards, to see clearly into pans on the stove, to read recipes, measure easily, and so on. A hanging ceiling fixture, some type of recessed fixture, or a large ceiling fixture that is not recessed may do the job best. Or, you may need a combination of fixtures. If you can't find the right solution, get some expert help. A badly lighted kitchen will never be a satisfactory kitchen.

Decorate Your Kitchen.   Plan the decorating of your kitchen just as you have the other rooms. Apply your knowledge of design principles and elements, and make use of color as you like. This is a room where you can let yourself go more safely than you can in any other room. Go back to Chapter Five, on floor coverings, and review the facts about resilient floorings. Check on practical wall coverings. The walls can and, if possible, should be, covered with a material that is grease- and moisture-resistant. It is best to use a truly washable wall covering. If you use paint, regular enamel is easy to wash, but if it seems too shiny, use a semigloss or, if you can get it, a dull enamel. You may want walls of wood, brick, or stone. If so, try to give them some kind of a dirt-resistant surface. The development of inexpensive, easy-to-maintain fabrics and wallpapers

Fig. 128 The kitchen in Fig. 127 shown in perspective.

has produced a much wider range of decorating possibilities for kitchens. Now, there is no reason why you shouldn't have curtains at every window and—if it appeals to you—wallpaper on some or all of the walls. Investigate drip-dry curtain fabrics and coated wallpapers that can be scrubbed clean.

Counters may be subdued or colorful. Many counters are covered with plastic laminates such as Formica and Micarta. These are very functional, but watch out for very hot pans and sharp knives. If you use this type of counter, it is a good idea to have an area of counter space of stainless steel or wood next to the stove. If you like a built-in chopping board, this is a good place for it. Linoleum is practical, if kept waxed, but it must be taken care of around a sink. If water gets under it, there will be trouble. Ceramic tile is a good counter surface and easy to care for, but it chips fairly easily and picks up dirt and stains where the surface is worn off. Some types of vinyl floor coverings are occasionally used on counters.

The decorating of your kitchen should be as interesting—and at least as much fun—as that of any other room in the house. If you have a large kitchen with some wall space away from the stove, you can make full use of pictures, plants, and other accessories. You may want a special "desk" counter to hold a telephone, cookbooks, menu plans, and grocery lists. Read magazine articles, look at other kitchens, and use your own imagination for additional ideas. Once you have a definite plan worked out and know just where everything will be placed, apply yourself to the use of color and pattern to make your kitchen one of the pleasantest rooms you have. If you want a gay kitchen, have it gay. If you want a quieter one that will seem more restful to you, design it that way. If you prefer a purely utilitarian one, you'll have no trouble planning that. But don't shortchange the appearance of your kitchen. After all, you'll probably be spending quite a lot of time there.

TELEVISION

Make the Best, Decoratively Speaking, of Your Television Set.　　Television has become an accepted part of most of today's homes. There has been definite improvement in cabinet designs, but a large television set is still an awkward piece of furniture, filled with a lot of heavy equipment that demands space. It is not a piece of furniture that should be featured in any room. Yet, for functional reasons, it must have an important place, with adequate viewing space conveniently located. Depending on the kind of set you have, there are a number of possible solutions.

If you are getting a large console model, choose a cabinet that goes as well with the design of your room as possible. If your room has a period influence, remember that when you make your selection. Try to get a wood tone that will blend with those you have. Once you have done that— or if you already have your set—the problem is one of arrangement. Work it out on your floor plan. Rearrange the furniture until you find a place where the set will seem as inconspicuous as possible, with seating arranged so that viewers can easily see the screen. Chairs on large casters or rollers, so they can be moved without effort, add to the versatility.

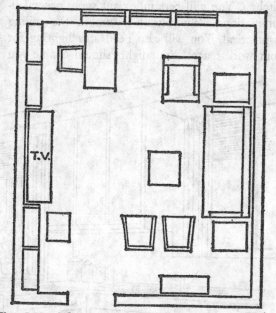

Fig. 129　This console television set is out of the way when not in use but easily viewed by a large group.

A portable set allows for more flexibility in a room. It may not be moved very far or often, but it does make it possible to arrange the room to function better for other purposes, when the television set is taken out. It is still a good idea to

Fig. 130 A built-in television set is easily accessible, but completely hidden when not being used.

work out your arrangement first on your floor plan, but you will probably find a solution easier than with a larger set.

Probably the most satisfactory solution, but also the most expensive, is the built-in cabinet. This can be made so that all equipment is out of sight and the screen covered when the set is not in use. The cabinet can be designed to fit the design of the room and can contribute to it instead of detracting from it. If you can't have a custom-built piece, perhaps you can fit your set into a piece of furniture you have, such as a bookcase or a cabinet.

If it is possible to have your television set in some room other than the living room, it should be put there. Not only does a set make your decorating problem more complicated, it also limits the use of the living room. Conversation, reading, games—all are difficult when a program is in progress. For the sake of family harmony, try to place your set where it won't annoy the members of the family who aren't interested.

A television set must necessarily be considered first on the basis of its function. Be sensible about that—but, unless you have a television room, don't let it dominate any room. If it must be in a room used for many other purposes, it will help if you can put the set out of sight and cover the dismally blank screen when it is not in use.

CHAPTER TWELVE

A SHORT HISTORY OF INTERIOR DESIGN

Following an extended period during which homemakers and designers seemed determined to create rooms that were either definitely traditional, or emphatically and often coldly modern, there has developed an eclectic blending of traditional design with contemporary furniture and modern architecture. You may or may not be interested in the design of the past, but since it

has had—and still does have—a tremendous influence, no book on the subject of interior design and decoration that ignores it would be complete. The periods that contributed design still in use, with either the original pieces or accurate reproductions, and those that had an influence on contemporary design will be briefly discussed.

ITALY

Baroque: roughly, 1550 to 1750. (Dates on periods often overlap and it is rarely possible to give them exactly.) The term baroque has been casually used, and is frequently misused. A French word (the contemporary period in France is called Louis XIV), it comes from the Portuguese word *barocco*, and here refers to an Italian period. The word *barocco* means an imperfect pearl, irregular in shape and asymmetrical, which accurately describes the design of this period.

Toward the end of the Renaissance, the reaction against the earlier restrained classicism in Italy resulted in this design that was totally unclassic, characterized by curved rather than straight line and by overornamentation. In its worst and most extreme forms, baroque was gaudy and ornate, and even the best, contrasted to the earlier classic design of the High Renaissance, was decadent.

But the better baroque design has many qualities that have kept its influence alive. It was an uninhibited, natural expression and had a wonderfully dynamic feeling of movement. It combined structural and decorative effects fantastically—and sometimes most impressively. Baroque design was large in scale, restless, opulent, and always dramatic. The domestic interiors of the wealthy people were splendid, with furnishings all on a grand scale—designed for effect rather than comfort. Plaster was used for a variety of decorative purposes—simulated draperies, cherubs, and many different kinds of scrolls. Marble was commonly used, or if there was no marble, wood or plaster was painted to look like marble. Colors were brilliant and contributed to the elegant effect.

Rococo: 1720 to 1760. The word rococo derives from the French word *rocaille*, meaning rock work, and *coquille*, meaning shell. The rococo design in Italy grew out of the baroque. They are often found together in a room or a building and it is sometimes impossible to judge which one dominates the style. The designs made profuse use of rock work and shells—both natural and stylized—foliage, flowers, and fruit, all kinds of scrolls, arabesques, ribbons, wreaths, and endless, flowing curves.

Rococo was smaller in scale than the baroque, with a more precious quality. The designs were never geometric—the circles were even drawn slightly oval. The finest development of the style was in France, under the reign of Louis XV. The Italians were not very careful about proportion, and sometimes used ornament with little regard for suitability. But many delightful rooms and pieces of furniture were designed and the style had great charm. It was often colorful, especially around Venice, with hues that were both gay and subtle.

FRANCE

Louis XIV: 1643 to 1715. This is the period during which the baroque style that started in Italy was developed in France. While the French artists and designers drew their original inspiration from Italy, they avoided the excesses and the restless, riotous qualities of the Italian baroque. The French style was unified by 1661, after Louis XIV came of age, and for the balance of his life it was strongly influenced by him. His main ideal was magnificence.

The architecture and furniture were both majestic—large in scale, formal, pompous, and very elegant. The furniture was heavy and masculine and the interiors were highly decorated. The lines were basically straight (unlike the Italian), but both the architecture and the furniture were covered with a profusion of carving, in which many geometric curves were used and which was often gilded. The ornament was intricate and combined a variety of motifs, such as acanthus leaves, masks, dolphins, garlands and festoons, scrolls, arabesques, and cartouches, with many flower and leaf forms. The King's monogram, two script intertwining L's, and his symbol—the sun—(with a face and spreading rays), were both frequently and conspicuously used.

Wooden walls, finished either in a wood tone or painted an off-white with gold moldings, were common. Tapestries, usually designed around allegorical subjects, were often hung on the walls. Heavy materials—brocades, brocatelles, satins, and damasks—were popular. Chairs began to be a little more comfortable. Bookcases became more common—developed from cupboards as more printed books appeared. Colors were strong, fairly dark, and sometimes brilliant—deep green, crimson, blues, and lots of bright, rich golds.

Louis XIV was the first European monarch to provide strong artistic leadership. Under the painter, Charles Le Brun, the arts were organized and the craftsmen given quarters in the Louvre. As a result of subsidization of artists of all kinds, and organization under strong leadership, France became the art center of Europe.

Regence: 1715 to 1723. During this period, France was ruled by a regent. Before the end of the preceding period, the style had started to change, and instead of the strongly symmetrical style of Louis XIV, the design gradually became asymmetrical. The richness of ornament of the earlier period was maintained for a while, but the design was lighter and no longer based on straight lines. It was a transitional time, the regence design evolving smoothly into the style of Louis XV.

Louis XV: 1723 to 1774. This French style is contemporary with the Italian rococo, but the design of the period in France was much finer. It was lighter than the Louis XIV, smaller in scale, gay, whimsical, feminine, and romantic. Although most of the design was asymmetric, some rooms were designed symmetrically, with asymmetric ornament. But even in the completely asymmetric design, the degree to which a feeling of balance was achieved and maintained, through optical balance, is amazing.

There were virtually no straight lines and most corners became curves. Design was based on a variety of beautiful, flowing, freehand curves, resulting in a graceful elegance that was typically French. Motifs were fanciful with great inventiveness of ornament. Designs, called *singerie*, showed the delightful antics of monkeys behaving like humans; others, called *Chinoiserie*, made use of and slightly ridiculed the Chinese influence. (Jean Pillement is a designer who made especially beautiful use of these themes.) Other motifs that were used in imaginative ways were palm leaves, all kinds of rocks and shells, flowers, flowing ribbons, garlands, doves, cupids, musical instruments, and the lozenge and cartouche.

Comfort was important, with everything scaled to convenient human use. Where the preceding period had aimed at the glorification of the king, the design of this period was intended for people, and majestic formality was replaced by intimacy. Small rooms for music or games, sitting rooms and boudoirs were planned for comfort and convenience. Chimney pieces of marble or carved wood were beautifully designed as part of a room. Rooms were often wood-paneled, finished in natural wood or painted in a soft tone with moldings of white or dull gold. In some of the more elegant rooms, the panels were filled with paintings by famous artists such as Fragonard or Boucher, or by less famous ones who copied their style.

The furniture was also designed on curved lines, with beautiful decoration—carving and elegant ormolu mounts. A fine chair leg of the period was created by combining several incredibly subtle curves. The chaise longue was introduced in a luxuriously comfortable version and widely used. Sofas, a variety of upholstered chairs (also comfortable caned ones), ottomans, and other special pieces (that we don't even have names for in English) were made. The furniture and the room had a flowing unity, the result of the beautiful rhythm of the design.

Velvets, damasks, satins, brocades, and some printed cottons were used. The patterns on the textiles were made up of curves, scrolls, ribbons, flowers, and the ever popular shell. Colors were pale—mauvy pinks, soft greens, putty tones, with white or gold. Some years before the death of Louis XV, a reaction started against all the curves which led to the return of classicism and the style of Louis XVI.

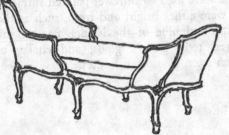

Louis XVI: 1774 to 1789. The transitional period started soon after 1760 and many of the pieces designed between that time and 1774 combined the curved and straight lines in a beautiful way. The Louis XVI style was a definite return to the classic. Straight lines were used, with curves that were controlled and usually geometric. The essence of the style, in contrast to the Louis XV, was its restraint. Rooms and furniture were still small in scale, feminine, and sentimental.

Wall treatments were symmetrical with the architecture balanced and orderly. Wood paneling was used, both in a natural finish and painted, and some walls were plaster, either painted or covered with wallpaper or fabric. Chimney pieces were usually of marble, beautifully proportioned and decorated simply with architectural detail. The excavations in Pompeii and Herculaneum in 1765 added to the classic influence. Decorative ornament used included classic running motifs such as rows of short fluting, frets, bead chains, and many other regular classic motifs such as rosettes, swags, festoons, pine cones, and urns. These were successfully combined with naturalistic contemporary floral arrangements, bouquets and baskets of flowers, sprays of leaves tied together with ribbons, and wreaths. Pastoral life, music, war, and love were themes used in designs carved or painted on panels.

The style was less elegant than the Louis XV, but comfortable and convenient. Beds were smaller, with beautiful wood frames showing.

Chairs often had oval backs or seat frames that curved softly across the front. Marble was frequently used for table or commode tops and leather was often used on writing tables. Commodes were simple in design and there were many of them.

Toile de Jouy, printed cotton with symmetrically placed scenes—usually pastoral and often in medallions—was very popular. Stripes and all-over conventional patterns, taffetas, damasks, and brocades were also in demand. Colors were soft and delicate—light blue, green-gray and pinky-gray, off-whites, and, though less often than before, gold.

Directoire: 1789 (Revolution) or 1795 (Directory) to 1804. This style was another transitional one, between the Louis XVI and the Empire, that was to follow. The same slender, refined forms and straight lines were used, but rooms and furniture were simpler and more severe, with less ornamentation. Backgrounds and design showed strong Pompeian influence. Some military ornament was used—drums, trumpets, spears, stars, and liberty caps—as well as many classic motifs. The designs were light, graceful, delicate, and in good proportion. Light fruit wood, ebony, and mahogany were popular woods, and more wood tones were used, with fewer painted surfaces. Colors were either bright and fresh, such as the red, white, and blue of the French flag, or subtle—grayed reds, greens, golds, and chalky blacks, taken from Pompeian houses.

Empire: 1804 to 1814. The full force of the classic revival was felt in this style which was influenced by Greek, Roman, Etruscan, and Egyptian forms. The two most famous architects of the period, on whom Napoleon depended heavily, were Percier and Fontaine. Napoleon was not at all artistic, but he realized the need for a solid, grand, and regal background to help in putting himself over as a great Emperor, and saw that such a setting was provided.

Absolute symmetry was the rule and the rooms were pompous, dignified, and masculine. Walls were of plaster—sometimes with painted decoration—or covered with wallpaper, or with fabric that was either stretched on the wall or draped in folds. The style was formal and cold and the furniture heavy. Severity completely replaced the intimacy and gracefulness of the earlier period. Marble mantels were classic, some highly decorated, others very plain.

Furniture was severe in the early part of the period and became more ornate later. While it was not as luxurious as that of the two latter Louis's, it was quite comfortable and convenient, although a little stiffer. Many different styles of chairs were made. Mahogany was the most popular wood, and much more of the furniture was painted than previously. Metal inlays of bronze and silver—some of them very beautiful—were often used. Tripod tables were made in imitation of those found in Pompeii. There were many commodes, usually decorated with metal mounts, and consoles were commonly used—often backed with mirror.

The decoration became increasingly ornate and gradually was overdone. Military motifs, such as victory wreaths, laurel, torches, and eagles, and exotic subjects such as winged sphinxes and winged lions, cobras, swans, obelisks, and Egyptian hieroglyphics were popular. Napoleon's own symbol, the bee, and his initial N, were used in the designs, and many old classical motifs were revived.

Color was important—bold but subtle. Wine reds, deep greens, grays, mustard yellows, golds, blues, and purples were all used. This period sparked the English Regency and the German Biedermeier, and its influence was felt in Italy and the United States. Authorities disagree on its aesthetic merits, since there was so much bad design, but many fine pieces have come down from the period.

French Provincial: There are no dates for this category because it does not represent a period, but rather a variation of period styles, particularly in the eighteenth century. The French periods just described are the court styles, seen in the various royal palaces and the smaller châteaux. French Provincial is an adaptation of the styles currently popular in court and city circles by the cabinetmakers and artists in the provinces.

During the reign of Louis XIII, provincial cabinetmakers began to produce their own version of chairs, with straw or wooden seats; stools, cupboards, and tables. Cupboards made at this time were particularly interesting, decorated with carving in geometric designs. These cupboards were still being made long after the reign of Louis XIII.

Because the design of Louis XIV was so definitely planned for the aristocracy and so sumptuous in character, little of it was adapted by provincial cabinetmakers, although some cupboards and simple armchairs were made. By the end of the reign of Louis XIV the lesser aristocracy and the wealthy merchants had increased in number and the court styles were modified for use in their own châteaux and homes.

The Louis XV rooms and furniture were designed for comfort and convenience and could be readily adopted by anyone, regardless of social position, who had the means to buy them. This style was very popular and retained its popularity in the provinces long after the period had "officially" ended. It accounts for a large share of the eighteenth-century provincial furniture in France, although by no means all of it. The Louis XVI style became fairly well liked in the provincial cities, but not a great deal of it was made for the village and country houses. There was little Directoire furniture made in the provinces and even less of Empire design.

Much the same kind of pieces were made in all the provinces—cupboards and sideboards of all kinds, tables, chairs, and benches, in particular. Beds featured in some homes were built into a room. The local influence varied—the difference usually being found in the design of the decoration or ornament—but in general, the designs of all the provinces were quite similar. Native woods were used; oak was especially popular—also walnut, elm, beech, and fruit woods.

The furniture was soundly and honestly constructed, and the rooms had an appealing kind of sincerity and a comfortable lived-in look. Although, on the whole, the designs for both interiors and furnishings were simple, less expensive, and certainly not elegant, fine pieces were made; many of them had great charm.

ENGLAND

William and Mary: 1689 to 1702. Although
little furniture of this period is to be seen today
outside museums, the period contributed a number of new pieces of furniture that, in one form
or another, are still in use today. William and
Mary ruled jointly from 1689 to 1702. Until the
beginning of their reign, they lived in Holland
and the style of the period has a definite Dutch
influence. They were a home-loving couple and
led a more domestic existence than many mon-
archs. Their way of life is reflected in the furniture which became lighter, smaller in scale, and
more comfortable.

Instead of the oak that had been popular, walnut became the favorite wood. Marquetry, wood
veneers, and lacquer were common. Forms were
basically rectangular, with both straight and
curved lines, and often some carved decoration.
(The style is contemporary with the later baroque.) Chair stretchers were flat and serpentine,
and often X-shaped. Queen Mary collected china,
starting a fad, and every fine home had wall
brackets and cabinets with shelves to display collections. The highboy, the kneehole desk, and the
slant-top secretary appeared during this period.
Several types of smaller, lighter tables replaced
the heavy refectory table, and a settee, which con-
sisted of two chair backs together, with upholstered seat, was introduced. Queen Mary and the
ladies of her court were excellent needleworkers
and the results of their handiwork were used on
chairs, which were upholstered and generally more
comfortable than those of earlier periods. Cane
was also used.

Grinling Gibbons, whose work continued into
the next period, was an outstanding wood carver.
His magnificent carvings enriched the architecture of many rooms and influenced all carved design.

Queen Anne: 1702 to 1714. Although this
was a short reign and the Queen herself had little interest in design, the design of the period is
exceptionally beautiful. The influence of the increased trade with the Far East was expressed in
the use of Oriental forms. The cabriole leg, introduced at the end of the previous period, was
widely used during this one. Beautiful curved
lines dominated the design. The scale was smaller,
but chair and sofa backs were higher. Small, upholstered sofas appeared. Chair backs were formed
to fit the human figure, with a center splat that
often resembled a violin and was called a fiddleback.

A high-backed chair was made with small wings
to protect against drafts. Windsor chairs were refined and made more comfortable. A greater variety of small tables was used, and secretaries replaced the huge, heavy chests. Lacquer was used
extensively as a finish, particularly on chests and
cabinets. China cabinets were still very popular.
Walnut was the most common wood in the first
part of the period, but toward the latter part,
more mahogany was used. Colors were influenced
by Chinese rugs and porcelains. The influence of
the period went far beyond 1714 and the transition into the lengthy Georgian period was a grad-
ual one.

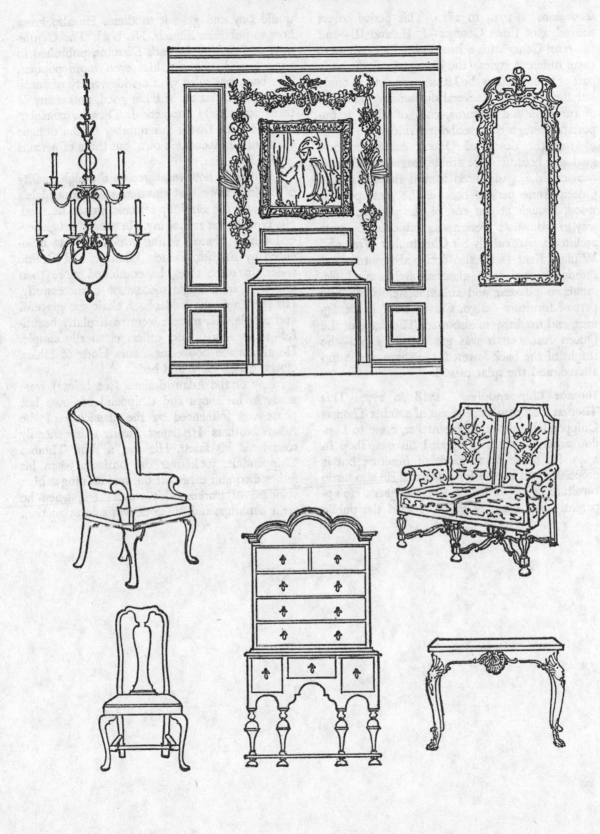

Georgian: 1714 to 1812. This period covers the reign of three Georges—I, II, and III—and the term Georgian is a broad one. Not only were there different styles (the change from the early part of the period to the latter was a marked one), but there were also several outstanding designers of furniture and interiors, each of whom is important enough to describe individually.

After the death of Queen Anne, furniture gradually became more ornate, larger in scale, and heavier. Mahogany, used toward the end of the Queen Anne period, became the most popular wood, though at the end of the period it gave way to satinwood. Design was influenced by great architects, particularly Sir Christopher Wren and William Kent (who also designed furniture and interiors), and such classical architectural elements as pilasters and columns were frequently part of furniture design. Carved lions' heads, figures, and masks were also used. The shape of the Queen Anne chair was gradually changed—the height of the back lowered, the shape of the top altered, and the splat carved.

Thomas Chippendale: 1718 to 1779. This Thomas Chippendale, the son of another Thomas Chippendale, also a cabinetmaker, came to London around 1727 and opened his own shop in 1749. He made many kinds of furniture but is especially well known for his chairs. He also made furniture in his shops for other designers. He apparently had a canny sense of what the public would buy and gave it to them. He also knew how to publicize himself. His book, *The Gentleman and Cabinet-Maker's Director*, published in 1754, served to make him even more popular. The book was filled with a wide variety of furniture designs, not all of them good, and many of them completely impractical. There is considerable evidence that a fair number of the designs were not Chippendale's own, but those of persons retained by him.

Authorities, however, agree on the high quality of cabinet work that came from Chippendale's shops, and the carefully selected woods he used. His favorite was mahogany. He went through several design phases, during which he was influenced by English, French, Chinese, and Gothic styles. In some cases, he combined more than one style in a single piece, not unsuccessfully. His version of the ladder-back chair was graceful and simple. His mirrors were particularly beautiful—some very ornate, others classically simple. He also made bookcases, many kinds of tables, clocks, desks, sofas, and beds.

Many of the Adam designs (see below) were made in his shops and Chippendale's own last phase was influenced by the classicism of the Adam brothers. His latest furniture is generally considered his finest. His son, a third Thomas Chippendale, took over the business when his father died and carried it on, maintaining a high standard of workmanship, until 1804 when he went bankrupt and his stock was sold at auction.

Robert Adam: 1728 to 1792. Robert Adam was the most famous of four brothers (the others were John, James, and William), all of whom were architects and designers. The strong influence of Roman classicism in his style was derived largely from a trip to Italy in 1754, during which he explored the ruins of Diocletian's palace in Dalmatia. He adapted classic ornament in a new and elegantly distinctive manner.

The brothers considered furniture design a part of the architect's trade and their furniture frequently has an architectural feeling. Furniture was designed as an important part of a whole decorative scheme, and often a room and everything in it, from the largest pieces to the hardware, was designed at one time as a single unit.

Their architecture was decorated with delicate, graceful designs done in plaster relief and painted over in soft tones. All motifs were classic and included festoons, vases and urns, scrolls, fans, fluting, medallions, drapery swags, lyres, and animal heads. The Adam brothers were not cabinetmakers and their furniture was often made in the shops of Chippendale or Hepplewhite (see below). They designed few chairs but are responsible for a variety of tables, cabinets, bookcases, and mirrors, and were the first to popularize the sideboard.

The furniture forms were mainly rectangular. Chairs, which often had curves in the shape of the back or seat, usually had straight, tapered legs. The furniture was decorated with motifs that were similar to those on the architecture; they were carved, painted, or applied. The colors most commonly used were soft grays, blues, mauves, yellows, and a gray-green that became known as "Adam green."

George Hepplewhite: Died 1786. There is little information about the life of Hepplewhite, but it is known that after his death, his widow, Alice, carried on his business under the name of A. Hepplewhite and Co. In 1788, she published a book attributed to him, called the *Cabinet-Maker and Upholsterer's Guide*. Probably few of the designs were actually his and there are no known authentic pieces of Hepplewhite furniture in existence, but his name represents a definite style.

Like Chippendale, he was especially well known for his chairs. His designs were generally smaller and more elegant than Chippendale's. His shield-back chairs are best known but he also made heart, camel, and wheel-shaped backs with central splats carved in urn shapes, ribbon patterns, and the Prince of Wales feather design. His chairs, like the Adams', usually had straight, tapered legs.

Hepplewhite made many kinds of small tables, sideboards, cabinets, and desks, decorated with low relief carving, inlay, or painted motifs. He worked with both mahogany and satinwood and used many other exotic woods for his inlay decoration. The style lasted until close to the end of the eighteenth century. He liked stripes on silks and satins, conventional designs, and soft, pale colors.

Thomas Sheraton: 1751 to 1806. A lay preacher and an inventor, Sheraton was self-educated and settled in London around 1790. In spite of his unquestioned ability, he lived in poverty. His first book, *The Cabinet-Maker and Upholsterer's Drawing Book*, was published in 1791. He was more a designer of furniture than a cabinetmaker, and while many of his designs are original, some were copied and others adapted.

His designs were as elegant and refined as Hepplewhite's, but he preferred straight lines to curves. He was famous for his Pembroke tables, he designed many dining-room and boudoir pieces, and was known for fancy cabinetwork with concealed drawers. His chair backs were usually rectangular, with more horizontal feeling than any of the earlier chairs.

Satinwood was his favorite wood and he used many exotic woods for veneers and inlays. He made little use of carving, preferring dainty, painted designs—flowers, festoons, and medallions. His later work, which was influenced by the French Empire, was inferior to his earlier designs. He liked silk with a floral pattern or stripes, often used toiles, printed chintzes, and linens. He frequently combined a soft blue with white or pale yellow.

English Regency: 1810 to 1820. The date for this style covers the brief period during which the Prince of Wales, later George IV (for an even shorter period), acted as regent for his father who had been judged insane. The influence of the period was carried on long after 1820, lasting until the time of Queen Victoria.

At the end of the eighteenth century, both in Europe and in England, there was a revival of interest in classic design. At this time, it was the heavier Greek and Roman design, rather than the Pompeian, that had the strongest influence. The Regency design of England, while it developed its own expression of the classic elements, was still greatly influenced by the French interpretation as seen in the Directoire and especially the Empire periods.

The Prince Regent was a gay blade who loved extravagance. The artificiality of the social background he created was sometimes reflected in the design, although many of the results were delightful. The Prince Regent is best known for the Royal Pavilion at Brighton, which he had built, then rebuilt and expanded into a fabulous collection of colorful, imaginative rooms, with a strong Oriental influence. The architect, John Nash, more than any other one designer, was responsible for the Royal Pavilion.

Other Regency design was, on the whole, more restrained. The early furniture was dignified and simple, strongly influenced by Greek and Roman classicism. These early pieces were also skillfully made. Construction was gradually cheapened and the later pieces are less fine in every way. They became cumbrous and were covered with a surplus of ornament which was often unrelated to the design of the piece of furniture.

Furniture designed for seating was, in general, rolled arms, many small upholstered settees and more comfortable than that in France. Sofas with chairs, and several different side chairs were made. Cane was often used. A variety of tables of all sizes, many of them with tripod or other types of pedestal bases, appeared. Bookcases, often made with copper-wire mesh covering the fronts, were used. Curves were common, frequently combined with straight lines.

Ornamental detail included cornucopias, honeysuckles, swans, acanthus leaves, lion masks, and animal legs and feet. Brass mounts and ormolu were often used. The favorite woods were mahogany and rosewood, and ebony and lacquer were common.

Thomas Hope was the most important designer of furniture, and he also designed some rooms. He published a book titled *Household Furniture and Interior Decoration* in 1807 that was widely used and had a strong influence on the design of the period.

Although there was less concern for proportion, both in furniture and architecture, many beautiful homes were built at this time. Walls were mostly plaster, with many pilasters and pediments, usually painted a contrasting color. Silhouettes were emphasized by strong value contrasts—light green, fawn, and terracotta, used against deep greens and rich browns. Black and gold were liberally used together. Carpeting in allover leaf-and-flower patterns was common.

Windows were hung with elaborate curtains, using deep swags, much fringe, and beautiful fabrics which were brilliantly colored—yellow, dark crimson, and purple—in velvets, satins, and damasks. Stripes were popular. For the first time, the house and garden were designed as a unit.

Victorian: 1837 to 1901. This long period is sometimes divided into Early Victorian: 1837 to 1850; Mid-Victorian: 1850 to 1875; and Late Victorian: 1875 to 1901. The furniture and architecture that were developed can hardly be described as a genuine style—more a confusion of styles. As the industrial revolution gained momentum, meticulous handcrafting gave way to machine-made furniture, with speed of execution becoming more important than high standards of design. Queen Victoria, herself, had no interest at all in art or design, and no other leadership appeared.

There was no genuinely original design. The early designs were adapted from the Regency but were so changed that they were difficult to recognize. The early furniture, made mostly of rosewood and mahogany, is usually considered the best. During the latter part of the Early Victorian period, there was a trend toward rococo. In the Victorian version, the curves became profuse and exaggerated and each piece was decorated, sometimes to excess, with carved fruit and flowers.

Other designs were borrowed or adapted from the Turkish, Gothic, Venetian, and Egyptian. Chairs usually had low legs and high backs, both usually curved, or were made in a Turkish or flamboyant Gothic design. Furniture was often fantastically carved with meaningless gingerbread ornament. The later furniture was made mainly of walnut. Gilt was frequently used. Upholstery was literally tufted, draped, buttoned, and corded. The effect was one of lavish display.

Forms were clumsy, badly proportioned, and heavy in scale. Rooms were high, with heavy architecture—heavy bolection moldings and marble fireplaces. Windows were tall, often covered with fancy lace under heavy satin curtains, sometimes hung from a deep, gold cornice. Machine-made carpets, with many colors, were used to cover the entire floor. The design of both room and furnishings was generally elaborate, overdone, and confused. There was rarely a unified effect.

William Morris (1836–1896), who is responsible for the Morris chair, had a more definite idea in back of his work than most designers of the time. He felt that it was important to combine materials appropriately for appearance and function in a piece of furniture or an interior. He promoted enthusiasm for medieval arts and crafts, and produced some interesting rooms, but his influence was not strong enough to have much effect.

The period was unquestionably a romantic as well as a sentimental one. The beauties of nature were revered and the floral designs in fabrics that were the result of this preoccupation with nature —especially flowers and leaves—were often beautiful, as were some of the wallpapers. Others were overdone. Papier-mâché was used for tables and even for chairs, often with mother-of-pearl inlay. Fringe, tassels, and an infinite variety of bric-a-brac (some of it with real character and charm) were profusely used. The what-not made its appearance to hold the bric-a-brac. Popular colors were shades of mauves and purples, with many different reds (including bright ones), greens, and gold.

UNITED STATES

Early American: 1620 to 1725. There was no consistent style in the colonies. The early settlers came to this continent from various parts of England and Europe, and from more than one social level. Some settled in New England, with its severe winters, others in the South where they found a much milder climate. All of these factors contributed to the variety of styles that developed.

All the colonists came on small ships and there was space for very little furniture. What they made when they got here was influenced by the few things that they did have and what they remembered. Shelter was the first need and the early houses were very simple, providing a minimum of comfort, convenience, or beauty. Furniture, built purely for function, was simple. The early houses were mainly of wood, which was readily available as the forests were cleared.

Except for rural Pennyslvania, where the German influence was strong (called Dutch because the early arrivals were misunderstood when they said they were "*Deutsch*"), and Charleston, where there were many settlers from France, the strongest influence was English. The furniture was provincial—plain and unsophisticated. In each colony it was made from whatever woods were available locally. Pine, oak, and maple were most common.

Usually designs from England appeared in the colonies about five years after they had become popular in England. There was a little delayed Jacobean, William and Mary, and considerably more of the style of Queen Anne, which was so well suited to the colonies that local craftsmen developed especially beautiful versions of it.

Appearance gradually became more important. As people continued to come from England, bringing some furniture, and books on furniture design, the cabinetmakers became highly skilled, adapting the designs and interpreting them in their own way to develop a style of their own.

The furniture in general was simpler than its counterpart in England, and more individual. Simple settees, cupboards (corner and hutch type), gate-leg, and butterfly tables, four-poster beds, and a variety of mirrors appeared as more emphasis was given to appearance and finer living. The stiff ladder-back chair was replaced by the more comfortable Windsor chair. Colors were cheerful—soft reds, yellows, blues, and greens—used with a lot of clean white. Fabrics were simple, many plain, or small, allover conventional designs.

Georgian: 1725 to 1780. Although there was some Georgian influence in the early part of the eighteenth century, the Queen Anne style remained popular until around 1760, when it was replaced by the Chippendale. As the struggle for survival decreased, more importance was given to design. There were still differences in design among the colonies, but in all of them, the homes were becoming less provincial and more elegant. Many of the houses were now made of brick or stone. The designs that continued to come from England were not followed closely, but interpreted by highly skilled craftsmen who gave them a definite character of their own. Interiors became much finer, more sophisticated, and, in many homes, quite luxurious. Mahogany was still the most popular wood.

By 1760, when the Chippendale style was in full swing, Philadelphia and Rhode Island were particularly known for the superiority of their designs and craftsmanship. The Philadelphia School was known for its beautiful highboys, chests, and chairs. William Savery (1722–1787) was considered by many the equal of any cabinetmaker working in London at that time. The Rhode Island School specialized in chests of drawers, cabinets, and desks. John Goddard and his son-in-law, John Townsend, became famous for their beautiful cabinet work.

Furniture was made with both straight and curved legs and various kinds of feet. Highboys, lowboys, tables—piecrust, tilt-top or pier—desks, canopied beds, and mirrors were beautifully turned out; comfortable sofas with loose cushions appeared.

Hepplewhite and Sheraton designs were also interpreted, toward the end of the period, with the same kind of individual flavor, reflecting both the maker and the location. Toward the end, also, there was the beginning of a classic revival. Hand-blocked prints were used, crewel embroidery, India prints, and elegant damasks popular. Colors were mostly soft, similar to those seen today at Williamsburg, with some emphatic accents of reds, greens, and browns.

Federal: 1780 to 1825. The Revolution interrupted the growing emphasis on elegance. After the war ended, a new style developed that was a combination of the native qualities that had appeared, French Empire, and English Regency. The Hepplewhite and Sheraton influence also continued into this period. The architecture and furniture had a feeling of classicism and were both finer in scale and simpler in design than the Georgian, which had become somewhat ornate near the end. The design, which represents the first years of the Republic, showed definite evidence of a national influence.

Two outstanding architects of the period were Charles Bulfinch and Samuel McIntire. Duncan Phyfe, who came to this country from Scotland, was the most important furniture designer. He was strongly influenced by Sheraton, but developed a style of his own. He used mahogany and some satinwood. The lyre form—used in a chair back, a table pedestal, or as a simple ornament—was a typical trademark of his design. He made many different pedestal tables, with curved legs, and a variety of chairs and sofas, with subtle curves in both legs and backs. Toward the end of the period, his work became heavier and somewhat decadent.

The eagle was a frequent Federal motif, used very decoratively in many different ways. Elegant fabrics were popular—beautiful damasks, brocades, and satins. Olive greens, light blues, and grays were used, sometimes with the colors of the flag.

American Empire: This is not actually a period, but a slight design trend that started toward the end of the Federal period and went a little beyond it. It is basically a combination of Federal and definite French Empire and the design was sometimes interesting, but inclined to be massive, not very graceful, and sometimes quite vulgar. The furniture made use of the round wood column and lion's paw feet found in the design of the French Empire, sometimes combined with the patriotic eagle and simple, homelike fruits, flowers, and horns of plenty.

American Victorian: 1830 to 1880. The design of this period was similar to the English Victorian, but even more of a hodgepodge. There were a few original designers at work but not enough to develop a distinctive style. Some interesting houses reflecting the influence of Gothic architecture were built in various parts of the country. The furniture was machine-made, as in England, and there were few fine craftsmen. One exception was John Belter, who used rosewood in a unique way and whose carvings were distinctive and beautiful.

Ostentation was more in demand than quality. The houses and the furniture had a genuine boisterousness that is endearing to many people. The what-not and the hassock appeared during this period and a wild assortment of bric-a-brac was used on the what-not. Shell and bead curtains, blackamoors, and much hand-done needlework were commonly found. Ornate fringes, tassels of all kinds, tufting, fancy trimmings—everything that could be added to a piece of furniture was used. As in England, reds, greens, golds, and some mauves, with heavy wood tones, were common. Designs made use of large roses and some very original and delightful floral wallpapers appeared.

GLOSSARY

Appliqué A French word meaning bracket, usually used in the decorating profession to refer to any kind of wall-lighting fixture.

Apron A flat piece of wood under and at right angles to a table top or chair seat, usually two or more inches deep. It is often shaped and usually slightly recessed.

Arabesque A kind of scroll pattern in which leaves, flowers, fruits, and geometrical forms are intertwined. Often used within a panel with lines of design following spiral direction.

Arcade A line of arches and their supporting columns—especially in hot climates—forming covered passageways over the sidewalk to protect people from the sun.

Arch A curved structure used as a support over an open space. Arches may be part of a circle, flattened, or pointed at the top. They are designed in a variety of proportions. The arch form is also used as decoration, either sunken in, projecting from, or painted on a wall.

Armoire The French word for a closet or wardrobe, usually furnished with a lock. Designed in the eighteenth century as a beautiful piece of furniture, it is customarily used instead of a closet in French homes.

Asymmetrical Not symmetrical. See *Symmetrical.*

Baluster A slender, turned column used as a support for a handrail. Balusters are sometimes also used as decoration.

Banquette The French word for bench has come to refer mainly to a long bench, placed or built against a wall. The built-in kind are commonly used in restaurants.

Bergère The French word for an upholstered easy chair, with solid sides and back and a decorative wooden frame showing. *Bergères* were first used commonly during the reign of Louis XV, when comfort became important in chair design. See also *Fauteuil.*

Bibliothèque Library—room or building—or a bookcase.

Blackamoor A statue of a Negro often colorfully and ornately dressed, in almost any size, used for a variety of decorative purposes, especially during the Victorian period.

Boiserie The French word for wainscot, the term is used in this country mainly to refer to wood paneling. The most beautiful *boiserie* was designed during the late-seventeenth and the eighteenth centuries.

Bolection Molding A molding that projects above the face of a surface—wall or woodwork—usually curving up to a rounded top member.

Bombé The word is the past tense of the French verb meaning to bulge or swell. The *bombé* design was most commonly used in commodes or the lower part of a desk, giving a rounded front. It was used more in the Chippendale, Louis XV, and rococo periods than any others.

Bouillotte The French word for kettle, this refers to a certain kind of table lamp, usually with three candles and a round, shallow, metal shade. The table on which it was used—round, with four legs and usually made with a gallery—is often called by the same name.

Cartouche The French word for cartridge, this refers to a scroll-like ornament, often an oval shape which was frequently used as the central motif in a design, and sometimes in the corner of a coved cornice.

Butterfly table A small table with drop leaves, supported by wing brackets somewhat in the shape of a butterfly, commonly used in the American colonies.

Cabriole A type of leg that curves inward from the foot and terminates at the top with a reverse curve. A very subtle kind of curve, used both in England and France in the eighteenth century.

Candelabrum (pl. Candelabra) or Candelabra (pl. Candelabras). A large, branched candlestick.

Casement window A window that is hinged at one side—may open in or out.

Chaise longue A French expression for a long chair that became popular during the eighteenth century. The chaise longue—often made in two pieces; sometimes three—is very comfortable for sitting or reclining.

Chimney piece See *Mantel.*

Chinoiserie The French expression for the adaptions of Chinese designs that were used to decorate wood panels, wallpapers, textiles, and furniture. See *Louis* XV in Chapter Twelve.

Classic Refers to design based in the artistic standards, principles and, methods of the ancient

Greeks and Romans—balanced, formal, austere, and usually simple and objective.

Commode   The French word for chest of drawers. Replaced the chests which opened from the top. Drawers made these chests much more convenient—the meaning of the word.

Composition   An arrangement of parts so as to form a harmonious and unified whole. (See the discussion of Unity in Chapter Two.)

Console   The French word for table or bracket. Originally, it referred to a bracket or shelf fastened to the wall; it now includes tables designed to be used against the wall.

Cornice   Originally the crowning member of an architectural composition. The term now usually refers to the horizontal molding that projects along the top wall of a room, or to a decorative band used to conceal curtain fixtures.

Cove   As part of a cornice, a concave curve between wall and ceiling.

Credenza   A cabinet that usually combines shelves and doors for storage. It was originally intended for use in the dining room but is now frequently used in living room, library, or hall.

Dado   The lower part of the wall of a room if treated differently from the area above it; usually has an ornamental border or paneling.

Decadent   Period of decline or deterioration in art or design.

Dormer window   A window set upright in a sloping roof.

Double-hung window   A commonly used kind of window made with two sections—one sliding down from the top, the other up from the bottom.

Drop leaf   A table with hinged leaves that fold down when not in use.

Eclectic   Selecting and using what seems best from various kinds of design.

Elevation   A flat, scale drawing of the front, side, or rear of a building or piece of furniture, showing no perspective.

Escritoire   French word for secretary or writing desk.

Façade   The face or front of a building.

Fauteuil   The French word for an armchair that is upholstered with an open space between arms and seat, as distinguished from a *bergère*, which is solid.

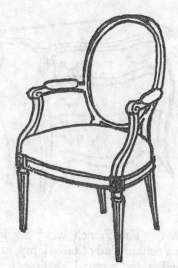

Festoon   A garland of flowers, leaves, or fruit, usually tied with ribbons and suspended in a V or crescent between two points. (See Swag.)

Fiddleback   The back of a chair, with a splat similar in shape to a fiddle; commonly used in the Queen Anne style.

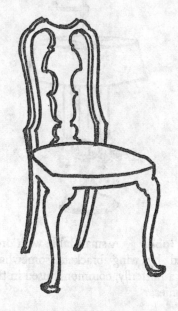

Finial   An ornamental terminal in the form of a knob; it may be a plain ball, pineapple, flame, or foliage, usually ending in somewhat of a point. On a lamp, it is used on the top of the screw that holds the shade.

Fireback   An iron lining for the back of a fireplace. It is intended to protect masonry and reflect heat and is often beautifully decorated.

Flock Paper   Wallpaper with a raised pattern, made of powdered wool. It has a soft, rather fuzzy surface.

Fluting   Shallow vertical grooves, usually parallel, used to ornament a surface. Often used on columns or pilasters in classical architecture.

Gallery   In furniture, a raised rim of wood or metal (often a railing in miniature) used on the edge of the top of certain pieces of furniture.

Gate leg   (or gate-legged) A style of table with drop leaves supported by legs which are folded back against the frame when the leaves are dropped.

Gimp   A flat, narrow, braidlike trim used as a finish on curtains and upholstered furniture.

Girandole   A candelabra with arms, often ornamented and usually forming a circle of light. (Comes from the Italian word *girandola* meaning a wheel-like cluster of fireworks.)

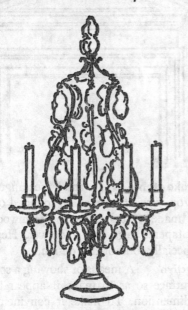

Grisaille   A style of painting that uses values of only one color, usually grays or soft, grayed browns. It generally gives the effect of plaster relief.

Highboy   A tall chest of drawers mounted on legs that make an important part of the design.

Hutch   A cabinet, dating from seventeenth-century England, with doors. Designed for storage; originally usually made of oak.

Inlay   A form of decoration made by setting pieces of wood, metal, etc., in a surface to make a design which is level with the surface when finished.

Kneehole desk   A flat-top desk with drawers at either side and open space for the knees in the center.

Ladder-back chair   A type of chair with a back that uses horizontal slats between the uprights, similar to a ladder.

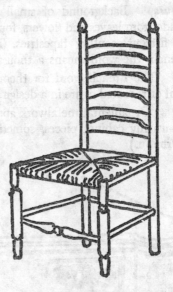

Love seat   Any small upholstered sofa—usually between four and five feet in length.

Lowboy   A small table with drawers, used as a wall piece. It often serves as the lower part of a highboy.

Lozenge   A diamond-shaped motif frequently used in decorative ornament.

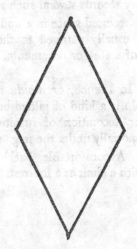

Mantel   The complete facing around the opening of a fireplace, including any shelf used above it as well as any part that projects from the wall.

Marquetry   A special kind of inlay used in fine veneer surfaces—from the French word meaning inlay or patchwork.

Medallion   A round or oval frame, usually containing a classic head painted or in relief or an ornamental motif.

Millefleurs   Background of small allover pattern made from leaves and flowers, found in many of the fifteenth-century tapestries. Taken from the French, the word means a thousand flowers.

Motif   The French word for theme, it means a central or repeated figure in a design.

Mount   Ornamental metalwork applied to furniture—usually cabinet pieces, sometimes chairs. (See Ormolu.)

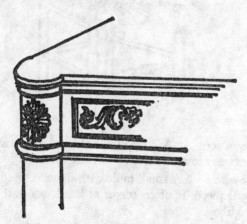

Neoclassic   A revival of the classic style and form. History records several such revivals.

Niche   A recessed space in a wall (often classic in design), usually planned to show or display some kind of statue or ornamental object.

Ormolu   In French, *or moulu* means ground gold. Ormolu is a kind of gilded bronze used extensively for decoration of furniture (elaborate mounts), especially under the reign of Louis XIV.

Ottoman   A comfortable, backless, cushioned seat; used with a chair as a footrest.

Panel   A surface, usually on wall or ceiling, set off from the surrounding surface by being raised, recessed, or framed.

Papier-mâché   A material made of paper pulp, mixed with rosin or oil, that can be molded.

Parquet   The French word for flooring or inlaid work, it refers to flooring that makes use of strips of wood in a geometric pattern.

Pedestal table   A table that is supported by a center base rather than four legs.

Pediment   Originally a low-pitched, triangular gable at the top exterior ends of a Greek temple, it has come to mean any similar form used in decoration of a doorway, overmantel, furniture, etc.

Pembroke table   A small rectangular table with drop leaves that may be rounded or squared (often made of mahogany or satinwood), with square tapered legs and a drawer. Hepplewhite was especially fond of this design.

Perspective   A means of showing a solid object on a surface so as to make it appear to have a third dimension. To make it convincing to the eye, sizes of distant objects are reduced; paralleled lines tend to converge.

Piecrust table   A table, usually with a round top, that has an edge that is raised, scalloped, or fluted; frequently a tilt-top table.

Pilaster   A flat rectangular feature, using the design of a column, but projecting only a few inches from the wall.

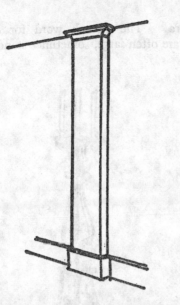

Plan   A drawing or diagram showing the arrangement in horizontal section of a structure or a piece of furniture—what you would see if it were possible to slice it through just above the bottom.

Plinth   A projecting piece at the base of a vertical column, pedestal, door trim, or any similar architectural part.

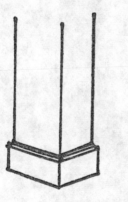

Refectory   Originally the dining hall in a monastery or convent, the word now usually refers to a long, narrow table of a design similar to those used in such dining halls.

Repoussé   The French word meaning to push away, *repoussé* refers to the relief work on thin metal that is formed by beating it from the underside.

Reproduction   A copy that is a close imitation or a duplication of an original design.

Restoration   The restoring or putting back into proper condition of anything that has been damaged from use or age—or both.

Side chair   A chair with a small seat (15" to 18" either side) and no arms.

Singerie   The French word for monkey trick, it refers to whimsical and elaborate designs based on the antics of monkeys in human poses.

Splat   The thin, flat piece of wood used in the back of a chair.

Stretcher   The name given to a wooden brace used between the legs of furniture. It may be flat, rounded, or shaped.

Stylized   A design that has been done according to the rules of a style rather than according to nature.

Swag   A decorative motif using a festoon of fabric, leaves, flowers, or fruit in a draped form. There are many variations and it is frequently used in plaster or carved in wood.

Symmetrical   Equal division of form, size, and arrangement of parts—identical halves.

Tambour   Usually refers to small slats of wood fastened together by means of a flexible backing, so they can be pulled back and forth across an opening. Taken from the French word for drum.

Torchère   The French word for candelabra. These are often large, sometimes standing on the floor.

Tester   The canopy on a four-poster bed.

Tilt-top table   A table with the top hinged to the base, so the top can be used upright.

Toile de Jouy   Refers to cottons printed at Jouy. (See Chapter Eight).

Tole   Painted and decorated metal, mainly tin.

Valance   A horizontal form, usually made of fabric or wood, shaped and hung over curtains at the top of a window, on beds, etc.

Veneer   A very thin layer of wood, usually fine-grained, bonded to a heavier piece.

INDEX

Accessories, 5, 7, 55, 72, 121–31, 140
Acetate, 105
 rugs, 65
Acrylic fibers, 106
 rugs of, 66
Activities, 27–28, 37, 39
Adam brothers, 158, 160
American design periods, 166–70
Apartments, one-room, 45–46
Area rugs, 69, 72, 74
Areas, 14, 16–17, 26, 55
Asbestos tile, 61–62
Asphalt tile, 60–61
Awnings, 91
Awning window, 90
Axminster weave carpet, 66

Balance, 5, 17–20, 37, 39, 55–56, 69, 80, 148
Baroque period, 156
 French, 146
 Italian, 144, 146
Barrel chair, 118
Baseboard, 30, 78
Basket weave, 104
Bathrooms, 61, 65, 85
Bedrooms, 39, 43–44, 55, 114
Beds, 150, 154, 158, 166, 168
Belter, John, 170
Benches, 109, 154
Biedermeier design, German, 152
Blinds, 91–92
Blueprints, 29, 31
Bolection molding, 78–79, 164
Bookcases, 41, 109, 114, 125–26, 146, 158, 160, 162
Books, 125–26
Boucher, 148
Breakfast room, 91
Brick flooring, 60–61
Broadloom carpets, 63, 67
Brussels woven carpet, 66
Budget, 27–28, 109, 118, 120
Bulbs, light, 134–35
Bulfinch, Charles, 170
Burlap, 105
Buying. See Shopping

Cabinets, 109, 114, 160, 168. See also Storage furniture
Cafe curtains, 94
Carpets, 60, 84, 105, 162, 164
 types of, 63–74
Case goods, 109–16
Casement curtains, 94–95, 106

Casement windows, 90
Center of interest, 7–8, 18–19, 22, 25, 41, 49, 63, 69, 78, 129–30
Ceramics, 125–27
Chairs, 14, 109, 111–12, 146, 148, 150, 152, 154, 156, 158, 160, 162, 164, 166, 168, 170
 types of, 116–19
Chaise longue, 148
Chenille carpet, 66–67
Chest of drawers, 114, 168
Chiffonier, 114
Child's room, 44–45
China, 126–27, 156
Chinese furniture, 110, 112
Chinoiserie, 148
Chippendale, Thomas, 158, 160, 168
Club style furniture, 118–19
Coffee tables, 109–12
Collections, 128–29, 156
Color, 5, 7–8, 13, 17, 19, 21–22, 24–27, 37, 47, 49–57, 78, 81, 84–85, 87, 105–7, 123, 129–30, 139–40, 144, 146, 148, 150, 156, 160, 162, 164, 166, 168, 170
 areas, 56
 chart, 50–52
 complementary, 52–53
 floor, 62–63
 names, 52–54
 primary, 49–51
 rug, 69, 75
 schemes, 53, 56–57
 secondary, 49, 51
 theories, 49–50
Commode, 114, 150, 152
Concrete floors, 60
Console tables, 111
Contemporary design. See Modern design
Contrast, 5, 19, 21–23, 39, 56
Cork tile, 60, 62
Cornice, 30, 77–78, 94, 97–98, 164
Cotton, 104–5
 rugs, 64–65
Curtains, 5, 92–101, 103, 105–6, 140, 162, 164, 170
 defined, 93

Dado, 30, 55
Decoration, 25–26, 144, 146, 148, 152, 156, 162
Denim, 104
Design periods, 5, 143–170
Design terms, 25–26
Desks, 109, 111–13, 156, 158, 160, 168
Dimensions, room, 29–30
Dining-living rooms, 46

Dining rooms, 39, 42–43, 109–11, 114
Directoire period, 150, 154, 162
Doors, 8, 18, 29–30, 77, 79, 90
Dormer windows, 90
Double-hung windows, 90
Draperies, 93. *See also* Curtains
Drawing rooms, 39
Dresser, 114
Drop-leaf tables, 111
Dual purpose rooms, 45–47

Early American period, 5–6, 166
Emphasis, 5, 21–23, 56, 78, 130. *See also* Center of interest
Empire period, 56, 152, 154, 160, 162, 170
    American, 170
End tables, 112
English design periods, 156–64
    furniture, 110, 112–14
Entrance hall, 39
Equipment, 27–28
European rugs, 68–69
Exterior appearance, 92

Fabrics, 5, 19, 23–25, 56, 72, 82–84
    curtain, 92–95, 97, 99, 105–6
    historical, 146, 148, 150, 152, 160, 162, 164, 166, 168, 170
    lamp shade, 137
    types of, 103–8
    upholstery, 105–6, 117–18
    valance, 98
    wall, 85–87
Family rooms, 41, 45, 55, 91
Federal period, 170
Felted fabrics, 103, 106–7
Fiber glass, 106
Fibers, 64, 104–6
Fireplaces, 7–8, 18, 25–26, 37, 40–41, 77–79, 148, 150, 164
    accessories for, 127–28
Fixtures, curtain, 100
Fixtures, lighting, 135
Flagstone flooring, 60–61
Flannel, 104
Flax, 104–5
Floor plans, 27–28, 31, 35, 37, 39, 42–47, 109, 118
    defined, 29–30
Floors, 7, 24–25, 55, 59–75, 139–40
    hard surface, 60–63
    soft, 63–75
Flowers, 128–29
Fontaine, 152
Form, 5, 8, 12–13, 17, 19, 25–26, 156, 164
Formal design, 8, 18, 39, 42, 131, 146, 152
Fragonard, 148
Framing, picture, 123–24
French design periods, 144–54
    furniture, 110, 112–14
French Provincial period, 154
Frisé, 104
Function, 3, 5, 26–28, 35, 37, 39, 41–47, 56, 62, 79, 85,

    87, 89, 93–94, 97, 100, 103, 107, 121, 134, 136, 140–41, 164, 166
Furniture, 5, 7–8, 27, 109–20, 129, 144–70
    American, 166–70
        arrangement, 28, 31, 35–42, 47, 79
    bedroom, 43–44
    children's, 44–45
    dining room, 42–43
    English, 110, 112–14, 156–64
    family room, 45
    French, 110, 112–14, 144–54
    guest room, 44
    Italian, 110, 144
    living-bedroom, 46–47
    living-dining room, 46
    living room, 42–43
    recreation room, 45
    scale, 31, 33–35
    study-guest room, 47

Game room, 148
Game tables, 109, 112
Georgian period, 158
    American, 168, 170
Gibbons, Grinling, 156
Glass:
    accessories, 127
    fiber, 106
    walls, 89
Goddard, John, 168
Greens, 128
Guest rooms, 42, 44, 47

Hall, entrance, 39
Handmade rugs, 67–68
Hanging, picture, 124
Hassock, 170
Headings, curtain, 99–100
Hemp, 104–5
Hepplewhite, George, 160, 168, 170
Highboy, 156, 168
History, design, 143–70
History, wall covering, 85–86
Hope, Thomas, 162
Hue, 52–53, 56, 144

Intensity, 52–56
Interior decoration defined, 25–26
Italian design periods, 144
    furniture, 110

Jacobean period, 166
Jalousie windows, 90
Jute, 104–5

Kent, William, 158
Kitchens, 28, 43, 45, 61, 65, 85, 91, 138–40
Knit carpets, 67
Knit fabrics, 103, 106–7

Lamps, 5, 121, 135–37
Lavatory, 28

Lawson style furniture, 118–19
Leather, 150
  accessories, 127
Le Brun, Charles, 146
Leno weave, 104
Libraries, 39, 41, 55
Light, 49, 56, 91–92
Lighting, 17, 37, 39, 43–45, 57, 79, 112, 122, 129, 133–37, 139
Line, 5, 8–14, 19, 21–22, 25–26, 55, 80, 144, 146, 148, 150, 156, 162
Linen, 104–5
Linoleum, 60–61
Living-bedrooms, 46–47
Living-dining rooms, 46
Living-guest rooms, 47
Living rooms, 39, 42–43, 114
Louis XIII, 154
Louis XIV period, 56, 144, 146, 148, 154
Louis XV period, 9, 12, 56, 137, 144, 148, 150, 154
Louis XVI period, 56, 150
Lowboy, 168
Luminosity, 54–55

McIntire, Samuel, 170
Marble, 60–62, 144, 148, 150, 152, 164
Marquisette, 104
Material. *See* Fabrics
Measurements, room, 29–31
Metal accessories, 127
Metal furniture, 109, 115–16
Milium process, 108
Mirrors, 14, 37–38, 43–44, 121–22, 152, 156, 160, 166, 168
Model rooms, 1
Modern design, 5, 18, 36–37, 100, 110, 113, 137, 143
Mohair, 104–5
Molding, 30, 78–79, 123–24, 148, 164
Morris, William, 164
Movement, 27. *See also* Rhythm
Music room, 39, 148

Nash, John, 162
Net, 104
Noise, 27, 64
Nylon, 105–6
  rugs, 65–66

One-room apartments, 45–46
Oriental rugs, 68
Ornament, 5, 24–26, 144, 146, 148, 150, 154, 160, 162, 170
Ottomans, 148

Paints, 56–57, 81–82, 139
Paneling, wood, 77–79, 86–87, 148, 150
Pantry, 28, 45
Parlor, 39
Parquet floors, 60–61
Pattern, 5, 7–8, 17, 19, 24–26, 56, 59, 62–63, 69, 73, 81, 83–85, 101, 107
Percier, 152

Periods, historical design, 5, 85–86, 143–70
Phyfe, Duncan, 170
Pictures, 5, 7, 14, 41, 121, 123–26, 130–31
  framing, 123–24
Pigment names, 53–54
Pile fabrics, 104
Pillement, Jean, 148
Plain carpets, 72–73
Plain weave, 104
Planning, 1–3, 27–28, 45, 53, 55, 77
Plaster, 144, 150, 152, 160, 162
Plastic accessories, 127
Plastic furniture, 109, 116
Play room, 28
Pleats, curtain, 99–100
Plush, 104
Plywood, 109, 114–15
Polyester fibers, 106
Porcelain, 126–27, 156
Pottery, 125–26
Proportion, 5, 14, 16–17, 39, 55, 63, 69, 79, 123–24, 127–29, 135, 137, 144, 150, 162, 164
  Greek Law of, 16–17

Queen Anne period, 156, 166, 168
Queen Mary period. *See* William and Mary period

Rayon, 105–6
  rugs, 65
Recreation room, 28, 41, 45, 55, 91
Regence period, 146
Regency period, English, 152, 162, 164, 170
Relief, 26
Reptition, 19–20
Rep weave, 26
Rhythm, 5, 19–21, 25, 39, 56, 63, 80, 148
Rococo period, 144, 148, 164
Rods, curtain, 100
Rooms, multi-purpose, 45–47
Rubber tile, 60, 62
Rugs, 5, 14, 60, 84–85, 103, 131
  types of, 63–75

Sales, 28
Saran, 106
Satin, 104, 107
Savery, William, 168
Scale, 5, 14–16, 25, 39, 44–45, 63, 69–71, 79, 84–85, 101, 123–24, 127–30, 135, 137, 144, 146, 148, 150, 154, 164
  drawing, 31–32, 35
Scotchgard process, 107
Scrapbook, 2
Screens, 87–88
Serge, 104
Settee, 156, 162, 166
Shades:
  color, 52–53
  roller, 91–92
Sheraton, Thomas, 160, 168, 170
Shopping, 27–28
  accessory, 129

fabric, 107–8
furniture, 109, 118, 120
rug, 69
Shutters, 91–92
Silk, 104–5
Singerie, 148
Slate, 60–61
Slip covers, 104, 106
Sofas, 112, 118–19, 131, 148, 156, 158, 162, 168, 170
Space, 25
Stairs, 64
Stoneware, 126
Stools, 154
Storage furniture, 109, 114–15, 154, 160, 166, 168
Study, 42, 46
Study-guest room, 47
Suitability, 55–56, 144
Swag, 94
Symbols, architectural, 29, 31
Symmetry, 130, 144, 146, 148, 150, 152. *See also* Balance
Synthetic fibers, 104–6

Tables, 14, 106, 109–13, 150, 152, 154, 156, 158, 160, 162, 164, 166, 168, 170
Taffeta, 104
Tapestry weave carpet, 67
Taste, 1–3, 26, 37
Television, 140–41
Terms, carpet, 64
Terms, design, 5–26
Terry cloth, 104
Textiles, 25, 103. *See also* Fabrics
Texture, 5, 17, 22–24, 26, 56, 73, 81, 123
Theme, 7
Tiebacks, curtain, 97
Tile, 60–62
Tints, 52
Toile de Jouy, 105
Tones, 52
Townsend, John, 168
Traditional design, 36, 39, 43, 143
Traffic patterns, 35–37, 41, 43–44, 79
Trim, 29–30, 77–78, 94

Trimmings, curtain, 100
Tufted carpet, 67
Tufted fabrics, 103
Tuxedo sofa, 118–19
Tweed rugs, 73
Twill weave, 104

United States design periods, 166–70
Unity, 2–7, 9, 16–17, 19, 22–23, 39, 52, 55–56, 59, 85, 101, 109, 124, 148
Upholstery, 104–7, 109, 116–18, 156, 164

Valance, 94, 97–98
Value, color, 52–53, 55–57, 81
Variety, 5, 9, 21, 23, 39
Velvet, 104
weave carpet, 67
Veneer, 109, 114–15, 156, 160
Venetian blinds, 91
Victorian period, 9, 12, 164
American, 170
Vinyls, 60–62, 82, 86–87, 107

Wallpaper, 5, 8, 19, 56, 72, 82–86, 139–40, 150, 152, 164, 170
Walls, 7, 18, 24–25, 41, 55, 105–7, 139–40, 146, 150, 152, 162
treatment of, 77–89
What-not, 164, 170
William and Mary period, 156, 166
Wilton weave carpet, 66
Windows, 8, 18, 29–30, 41, 77, 79, 164
types of, 89–101
Wood, 144, 150, 152, 154, 158, 160, 162, 164, 166, 168, 170
accessories, 127
Wool, 104–6
rugs, 64–66
Woven carpet, 66–67
Woven fabrics, 103–4, 107
Wren, Sir Christopher, 158
Writing table, 109, 150